oN
Call

Stuart
Buchanan

EXPLORING GOD'S LEADING TO CHRISTIAN SERVICE

oN
Call

Stuart
Buchanan

EXPLORING GOD'S LEADING TO CHRISTIAN SERVICE

Text copyright © Stuart Buchanan 2001
The author asserts the moral right
to be identified as the author of this work

Published by
The Bible Reading Fellowship
First Floor, Elsfield Hall
15–17 Elsfield Way, Oxford OX2 8FG
ISBN 1 84101 215 7
First published 2001
1 3 5 7 9 10 8 6 4 2 0
All rights reserved

Acknowledgments
Unless otherwise stated, scripture quotations are taken from The New Revised
Standard Version of the Bible, Anglicized Edition, copyright © 1989, 1995 by the
Division of Christian Education of the National Council of the Churches of Christ
in the USA, and are used by permission. All rights reserved.

Scripture quotations taken from the Holy Bible, New International Version,
copyright © 1973, 1978, 1984 by International Bible Society, are used
by permission of Hodder & Stoughton Limited. All rights reserved.
'NIV' is a registered trademark of International Bible Society.
UK trademark number 1448790.

Scripture quotations taken from the New Jerusalem Bible, published and copyright
© 1985 by Darton, Longman and Todd Ltd and les Editions du Cerf, and by
Doubleday, a division of Bantam Doubleday Dell Publishing Group, Inc., are used
by permission of Darton, Longman and Todd Ltd, and Doubleday, a division of
Random House, Inc.

p. 52: 'Here am I' from *Heaven Shall Not Wait* (Wild Goose Publications, 1987)
words by John L. Bell & Graham Maule
copyright © 1987 WGRG, Iona Community,
840 Govan Road, Glasgow G51 3UU, Scotland.

A catalogue record for this book is available from the British Library

Printed and bound in Great Britain by Omnia Books Limited, Glasgow

Foreword

'On call' is a term that is well understood by the emergency services, health professionals and many who work in Social Services. It also applies to many in pastoral ministry in local churches. But does it apply to ordinary Christians doing ordinary jobs in business, commerce or a profession, or caring for toddlers at home?

Stuart Buchanan provides us with a stimulating examination of what the Bible reveals about being 'on call' in the Kingdom of God. He opens windows for us on the biblical narratives that show how God calls ordinary people into his service to do different things at different times. Often his interpretations of well-known stories are fresh, vibrant and challenging. Sometimes they challenge the accepted view and provide novel ways of understanding the text. However, they are always valuable and written in an interesting style. Many of the illustrations and examples are taken from Stuart Buchanan's work with the Church Mission Society and the Anglican Communion. However, this book will be of value for all Christians, whatever their church affiliation. For those already serving somewhere in the world, it could be a refresher course in re-examining their calling. For those starting out on a voyage of discovery in seeking to know God's will for their lives, it will be a valuable resource that will reward the careful and prayerful reader. I thoroughly recommend this book to all Christians involved in God's mission to the world. I guarantee it will inform, stimulate and often challenge you to think about your faith and service in new ways.

Stanley Davies
Global Connections

Church Mission Society (CMS)

The Church Mission Society (CMS) is actively involved in sharing God's love with the people of Africa, Asia, Britain and Eastern Europe. CMS was established in 1799 as a voluntary society of the Church of England but works with many different Churches and Christian groups around the world.

Historically, it provided missionaries to help to establish the Anglican Church in many parts of the world. Today we send mission partners, co-workers with local churches, sharing in evangelism, leadership and theological training, church growth and community development.

CMS works to support pioneering evangelistic work and to establish and support churches in places where there are few or no Christians, sensitively sharing the Christian faith with those of other faiths or none. It also works for justice, peace and reconciliation and encourages holistic initiatives in community development and health care.

Contact CMS at:

Church Mission Society
Partnership House
157 Waterloo Rd
London SE1 8UU

Tel: 020 7928 8681
Fax: 020 7401 3215
Website: www.cms-uk.org

Contents

Introduction

Nearly two thousand years before the birth of Christ, according to the Bible, a man called Abram sensed that God was setting him aside and wanting him to move from his home to a different country to carry out a special task. The Bible records events that occur over the next two thousand years and, as we read through these events, we find that this experience of believing that God is wanting you to move, or to perform special tasks, is repeated again and again.

Two thousand years after the birth of Christ, people are still experiencing such a sense of leading to move, to specific types of ministry or to perform particular tasks for God. For the last twenty years, I have been privileged to help people explore the sense of leading that they have and to hear how they have perceived God communicating with them and directing them. Within my own faith journey I have tried to relate their experiences to the Bible, and my reading of the Bible to the stories that I have heard.

The writers of the different parts of the Bible generally describe the experience of perceiving that God is communicating with an individual as God 'speaking' to that person. If we read the Bible looking for a simple formula, so that we can be absolutely sure whether or not God is speaking to us, then we will be deeply disappointed. Usually the authors conclude that 'God said...' and leave us with no hints about how the hearer perceived that they were experiencing a word from God. When we begin to look more deeply at some of the passages, we realize that God can speak to these people in very different ways.

During the last twenty years, I have noticed that Christians have gained a far greater self-awareness and understanding of how they function. Many might have explored their personality, trained in counselling or received counselling. One example of the different ways in which people function is that some are more likely to perceive their encounters with God as happening within themselves, while others experience God in what is happening out in the world. I have tried, in response to this, to balance the chapters of this book between the response to the inner voice and the response to God speaking out there in the world. The final chapter is an attempt to draw these approaches together.

It is also clear that the ways in which people process their experiences are different. Some will have an eye for the details and others for the big picture. Some, in processing their experiences, will be in touch with their emotions and senses, and will conclude that 'they feel...'. Others will find that it is a cerebral process and conclude that 'they think...'. The end results of processing experiences will be perceived differently: for some there will be a definite conclusion and for others it will be more open-ended.[1]

Our Christian backgrounds, our previous recollections of God at work within our lives and our experience of Church will influence how we expect God to communicate with us. For some the most authoritative voice will be the voice within that is perceived as God speaking directly to them; for others it will be the local church; for others the authority will be the wider body of the Church. Each person will hold together different balances between these three influences.

The fact that encounters with God might be experienced differently depending upon culture is not a new discovery, and will be explored further within a later chapter. That different age ranges within a particular culture will have different sub-cultures that affect their understanding of God's leading is a more recent discovery, with which those involved in testing vocation are only just beginning to grapple.

Personalities were just as diverse in biblical times as they are now, and the Bible is about people within different cultures and of different ages. My starting point is not with an analysis of different personality indicators, or an understanding of Generation X,[2] but with different biblical characters. In looking at these characters, I will expect to find diversity because God does create people differently. He does so because he has different tasks to be done, which will need different types of people to do them. I hope that some of these examples will have something to say to you.

9

If God has created different types of people, then the Church has responded to this by creating all sorts of different types of ministries. The different denominational churches will have different terms to describe different types of clergy. Within the Church of England alone, the biblical trio of bishop, deacon and presbyter (later to be known as priest) has been augmented with terms like archbishop, archdeacon, curate, dean, locally ordained minister, non-stipendary priest, prebendary, provost, rector, rural dean and vicar. There are ministries within the religious communities and there is a wealth of lay ministries, some full-time and some part-time: Church Army, lay worker, parish evangelist, pastoral auxiliary, Reader (formerly Lay Reader) and youth worker. I am sure there are Church of England ministries that I have missed, and each denomination will define different ministries in different ways. Meanwhile, the mission agencies each have their own range of different programmes offering opportunity for ministry.

There is a whole high street of spiritual supermarkets out there, offering their diverse ministries. Some people will have a deep sense of commitment to one particular denomination or one particular mission agency, the spiritual equivalent of the supermarket 'loyalty card'. Even if you have such a 'loyalty card', committing you to using the 'supermarket' of one church or mission agency, you can still find a dazzling array of ministries on offer. Like items on supermarket shelves, these ministries will be packaged in different ways. Some churches and agencies will have done more to promote their ministries in attractive ways. Some ministries are offered on websites, and the attractiveness of the website can easily influence the surfer. There are booklets and brochures, produced annually, which give overviews of the ministries on offer. Some will describe the whole breadth of what is available within a particular denomination or mission agency, and others will tell you more about which agencies or churches offer variations of a particular type of ministry, or offer possibilities within particular countries.

I offer what follows as an attempt to make sense of the stories of some of the people who are called within the Bible, as a way to understand better what they were called to, the nature of the one who called them and the implications for us today. Whilst my own experience has primarily been in testing the vocation to cross-cultural opportunities, usually within another country, I have often helped people to find their vocation within their own country. I hope that much of what follows will still be relevant to anyone who is exploring a sense of leading to any Christian ministry. I hope it will equip you to know the questions that you will need to be asking of yourself, and of the ministry that you may wish to explore, in testing your own sense of God's leading.

NOTES
1 The Myers-Briggs indicators are not the only way of looking at personality, but they are indicators that more and more Christians are familiar with, so the examples given here are based upon them.
2 A term that has been used to describe those who have been born since the early 1960s.

CHAPTER 1

Called to what?

Before we consider any of the biblical examples, a question: how do you feel about the idea that God might speak to people today? OK, so this is a Christian book and Christian authors write about such issues, and you are unlikely to have picked up this book if you did not believe that it was possible for God to speak. Step outside that understanding for a moment, and ask yourself the question again. Suppose you switch on the radio or the television and catch the last few words of a news item: '...*he said that he had done this because God had told him to.*' If you are at all like me, then your heart will drop at these words. Surely, you think, some atrocity has occurred and the perpetrator is justifying his action by putting the blame upon God. Worse still, not for any victim but for me and my Christian faith, someone with a high profile and who claims to be a Christian might be explaining away their sexual or other misdemeanour.

Alternatively it might be a historical programme about the Crusades or the Spanish Inquisition, or some other atrocity that was carried out because some Christians thought that God was telling them to do so. If God, allegedly 'speaking' to someone, makes the national or international headlines or a documentary, then it tends to be bad news, and I tend not to believe that it involved the God who is the Father of our Lord Jesus Christ. If the event is only newsworthy within a local Christian community, then it might be good news, and it might well be something that I believe is of God. It is a sobering thought that the theological colleges and Bible colleges are not the only places full of those who believe that God has spoken to them—the psychiatric hospitals and secure prisons have their share as well. Concluding that God has spoken to you can be a risky business.

What criteria do we use in deciding whether or not it really was

God speaking in any of these situations? Personally, I would want to know what it was that the person *did*. Is their action compatible with a response to the God who loved the world so much that he sent Jesus Christ? We can use the Bible as a starting point in beginning to measure this, but we still need to be careful. If we look at individual texts, particularly in the Old Testament, we might still be able to justify all sorts of actions. It is important to look at individual texts and accounts in the light of the whole of the biblical message. We should be doing this prayerfully, in the hope that the Holy Spirit will guide us in our understanding.

So, with that caution in mind, let us start by asking what it is that God calls people to *do* within the pages of the Bible. When we have answered that, we can ask ourselves how any specific type of present-day ministry might fit in.

A good starting point is to look at the first person that God calls. God's first initiative in mission was the calling of Abram, later to be known as Abraham. If you are being called to mission or a ministry, then you are being called in the same tradition as Abraham and all those who followed him in obeying God's call in the Bible. I would suggest that the task of the modern Christian follows on from the task that Abraham was called to. Let us begin by exploring what it was that Abraham was called to do.

Although God makes different promises to Abraham, the all-embracing one is found in Genesis 12:3. Here, God promises Abraham that 'in you all the families of the earth shall be blessed'. If we are called in the tradition of Abraham, then we are called to be a blessing to the nations. What a wonderful thought. Within the Anglican ministry, who can and who cannot *give* a blessing is carefully defined, but to *be* a blessing is another matter. However, before we get carried away with the idea of being a blessing to the nations, we need to test the idea out. Does it stand up? Does it fit with what the rest of the Bible is saying?

In Luke 24:27, when the risen Jesus met the two disciples on the road to Emmaus, he talked them through *Moses* and *the prophets*. The original readers of these words would have recognized the term

'Moses' as meaning the first five books of the Old Testament, and 'the prophets' as meaning the history books and the books that we would consider as being the prophets. It is a shame that Luke did not give us more detail about Jesus' overview of the Old Testament. If he had, I could have referred you to it. Instead I need to take you through my own lightning tour of the Bible. I want you to imagine that you are reading the Bible for the very first time. I want you to ask yourself the type of questions that you would ask as you begin to read any book the size of the Bible.

A biblical overview

Who is this book about? As I read the first few pages, I see that it is about God and about the whole of his creation. I then come across Adam and Eve and then their descendants. As I progress through Genesis 1—11, I read about a God who is relating to all the families of the earth. By the end of chapter 11, the Bible is referring to all the nations of the earth. I begin to conclude that this book is about God and his creation, and about all the nations of the earth. Then I move on to chapter 12 and the emphasis changes. It now appears to be about an individual called Abram and then about his descendants who become a nation known as Israel. Before trying to make sense of *what* this book is about and what its message and relevance are for me today, I want to know *who* it is really about. Is it about God and the nations, or God and Abraham, or God and Israel?

I don't know what you do when you have this problem of not knowing who a book is about, but I cheat! I look at the back page, or at least the last few pages. By doing this, I can find out who the story is really about and I can concentrate on those characters as I read the book. So, then, if we jump ahead to Revelation 21 and 22, we see that the Bible ends with God's relationship with his new creation—all the families of the earth, all the nations. The Bible *starts and ends* with the relationship between God and his whole creation, all the families of the earth, all the nations.

Called to what?

Those first eleven chapters of Genesis tell us about God creating the heavens and the earth and about something going wrong between God and his creation. It is at that point that this wonderful, loving God takes the initiative and sends Abraham to be a blessing to the nations. Abraham is given the task of putting things right again between God and his whole creation. As we read through the Old Testament, looking for how the stories relate to this bigger theme of God and his whole creation, we see that Abraham eventually fathers Isaac and, as the chapters and the centuries go by, his descendants become a nation, Israel.

More centuries and chapters pass, and Israel becomes established in Palestine. What a choice of location! God has not only called Israel to be a blessing to the nations but has strategically placed them where the surrounding nations cannot help but trip over them or bump into them. Situated at one end of the Fertile Crescent, with the sea to one side and deserts in other directions, many of the known trade routes came right through the land. Through the experiences of the Exodus and the wilderness, God tries to shape Israel into being a model nation. Israel is called to be an example and a witness to the nations. In this way they should become a blessing to the nations, bringing the nations back to God. A thousand years before Christ, Israel reaches its pinnacle during the reigns of King David and King Solomon. The surrounding nations take notice of Israel and its monotheistic faith. After that, with a few reversals, it is downhill all the way. There is a split into two different, and often rival, kingdoms of Israel and Judah.

As I read further, through 2 Kings and 2 Chronicles, I begin to lose sight of Israel's role as a blessing to the nations. Israel, the northern kingdom, is attacked by Assyria and many of its people are taken into exile. The Assyrian occupiers move other peoples on to the land instead. Those who are left intermarry and lose their identity as a Hebrew nation. Their descendants become known as the Samaritans. The southern kingdom of Judah is also defeated by Assyria, but not exiled. As Assyria loses its power, it loses its hold over Judah. Judah has learnt some lessons from the experiences of Israel but, a hundred years later, these lessons have faded and the behaviour of the nation is just as bad as ever. By now, Babylon is the dominant nation and Judah succumbs to her power. Most of the people are taken into exile in Babylon, and the temple is destroyed, along with most of Jerusalem.

The nation of Israel is elect. It has been chosen for a task, for responsibility. But Israel falls into the trap that exists for all those who are elect. Israel thinks that it has been chosen for privilege instead of responsibility. Through much of the Old Testament, there is an emphasis upon Israel keeping itself separate from the nations so that it should not be contaminated by them. During the period of exile in Babylon, the people begin to reflect on the nature of this election. A deeper understanding develops, of Israel having a special purpose rather than special privileges. The prophet Isaiah sees Israel as a suffering servant, called to suffer on behalf of the nations in order to be a blessing to the nations. Isaiah's thinking is summed up in the beautiful language of the four Servant Songs: Isaiah 42:1–9; 49:1–6; 50:4–9; and 52:13—53:12.

As Isaiah helps the exiled people to understand their calling to be a blessing to the nations, he also sees how God will act to bring about their own liberation. Babylon is on the wane and Persia is on the ascent. The Persian ruler King Cyrus releases the exiles and encourages them to return and also to rebuild their temple. Some return and the temple is eventually restored, but there is a renewed emphasis on trying to remain pure and separate from the nations.

The prophet Jonah can be seen as an image of Israel—a reluctant missionary who runs away rather than taking God's message to another nation. The writer of the book of Jonah tells us that God wants the other nations to repent and turn to him. He also shows that, with God's help, the task is not difficult. A reluctant Jonah witnesses successfully not only to Nineveh, but also to the sailors on the boat that he uses to escape.

The return to Judah and the rebuilding of the temple in Jerusalem are followed by invasion by the Greeks. Whilst the Babylonians had allowed freedom of worship and Cyrus had encouraged the rebuilding of the temple, the Greeks tried to force their culture and religion upon those whom they conquered.

By the time Jesus is born, Greek rule (which is the background to the two books of Maccabees) has given way to Roman rule, and the golden age of King David is a distant memory from a thousand years before. The emphasis is upon survival and, as for many who struggle to survive, there are deep differences among the Jewish people in understanding how this should happen. Some compromise or collaborate with the ruling power, and others keep their distance. Some are looking forward to the 'Day of the Lord', as predicted in the book of Joel—a time when God's reign will be a direct reign upon earth. Many expect that God will send a Messiah, probably a military leader, to throw out the Romans. Some go about their everyday lives as they wait, and others retreat to form uncontaminated communities in the desert. The idea of being a blessing to the nations has been lost completely.

As we move into the New Testament, the change is as sudden as it was when we moved from chapter 11 to chapter 12 of Genesis. Then we moved from the nations to an individual, and this time we move from the story of one nation to a new individual, Jesus. The Gospels are an account of his life, ministry and death, resurrection and post-resurrection appearances. As we read through Matthew, we experience *déjà vu*. We read about the flight into Egypt and, later, a baptism in the Jordan seems to replace a crossing of the Red Sea as a prelude to a period in the wilderness. It comes as no surprise, as we read the events of the Passion, that those four Servant Songs in Isaiah seem to be describing Jesus.

John structures his Gospel differently. Jesus becomes the fulfilment of the different Jewish feasts. The Old Testament is rich with imagery, and that imagery is echoed in the Gospels. Particularly in John's Gospel we see Jesus as the bread of life, as the water of life, as the vine, as the shepherd.

The relevance of Jesus to the nations can, at a first glance, seem as hidden as this blessing was in the Old Testament. Some of his words, such as those given to a Canaanite woman in Matthew 15:24–26, seem to deny a wider role, but the representatives of the nations are there at two key events. In Matthew 2:1–12, we read of wise men arriving from the east to pay homage to the newly born Jesus. In John 12:20–26, the arrival of some Greeks who wish to speak to Jesus is the sign to Jesus that the events of his Passion are about to begin.

One of the promises that God had made to Abraham was about 'the land'—the territory promised to his descendants. A messianic expectation was that God would return this land, and political and military control of the land, to Israel. Jesus does not refer once to the land during his ministry. Instead, the theme that he develops is the Kingdom of God. The final discussion between Jesus and his disciples, according to Acts 1:6–8, is immediately prior to the ascension. They ask him about the restoration of the Kingdom to Israel—by which they mean the land itself. In response to this question about the land, Jesus talks once again about a broader understanding of the Kingdom—a kingdom that is for all of the nations. All of the Gospels end with Jesus commissioning his disciples to go and witness to the nations.

God's plan for redeeming the nations starts off concentrated in one person, in Abraham. That calling is passed on to Abraham's descendants, and the whole nation of Israel then takes on the calling to be a blessing to the nations. After the reign of King Solomon, the nation splits into two kingdoms, then Israel is destroyed and the focus remains with Judah. Judah is taken into exile and only some of the people eventually return to the land, the remnant referred to in 2 Kings 19:30–31. God's purpose is focused on an ever-decreasing number of people until we find it centred entirely on one person, Jesus. Jesus is the one who has taken on the mantle of Israel and who will bring a blessing to the nations. He is the one who fulfils the prophecies made by Isaiah about a suffering servant who suffers on behalf of the nations.

But the Bible does not end with the Gospels. As we move into Acts, we find that the story is no longer about Jesus, but about his followers. If parts of the Gospels seem to echo themes from parts of the Old Testament, then the Acts of the Apostles has parallels with the book of Joshua. As Joshua consolidated the land, so the early

Christians consolidate their numbers. It looks at first as if the gospel of Jesus will only be shared with the Jewish people, and the rest of the nations will again be forgotten. At last, however, the gospel is taken to the nations. Acts tells particularly of the roles of Paul and Barnabas in this task. According to tradition, Mark took the gospel south to Egypt, and Thomas took it east, possibly as far as India. Acts ends with Paul having arrived in Rome. Although he is in prison, he is at the centre of the economic and political power that controls the known world. The rest of the New Testament consists of the letters sent by some of the leaders of the early Church. These letters address the issues faced as the Church grew, developed, expanded into the nations and engaged with issues found within both Jewish and Gentile cultures.

Jesus has passed on the task of being a blessing to the nations to the Church. We will probably be familiar both with the initiatives that brought the gospel to Western Europe, and with the Protestant missionary expansion from Europe during the last three centuries. Between the biblical era and the modern era, the blessing has still been taken to the nations. The gospel spread north, through the Balkans, finally arriving in Russia just over a thousand years ago. Thomas took the good news east, and either he or his followers founded a church in parts of India. The expansion to the east saw the gospel shared as far afield as China by the seventh century. The Portuguese and Spanish colonial expansions commencing at the beginning of the 16th century again took the gospel to India and China, as well as to the Americas and Africa.

So, we can see that the original call to Abraham to be a blessing to the nations does fit with what the rest of the Bible is saying. Indeed, it is central to the whole message of the Bible, from Genesis to Revelation. Despite decreasing church attendance in the West today, that task of being a blessing to the nations continues. If we are part of the Church, we are part of that task and part of the biblical story that we have just surveyed. We might be called by God to specific tasks and specific places, but all of us, as part of that bigger calling to the Church, need to be ready and waiting for whatever God wants us to do. Basically, we are all on call.

A blessing to the nations

So we are called to be a blessing to the nations. Being a blessing sounds very positive and affirming, but what does it really mean? What do we need to do to be part of that blessing? The answer lies in the task of putting right what has gone wrong in the first eleven chapters of Genesis. The biblical shorthand for the thing, or things, that have gone wrong is the word 'sin'. I always feel that sin is one of those words that we are meant to understand but that no one explains properly. As we look at the stories of Adam and Eve, Cain and Abel and the tower of Babel in the first eleven chapters of Genesis, we see that they all have the same starting point. There is a breakdown in the relationship between God and the individual person. This breakdown has various causes: disobedience and thinking that we know better than God (Adam and Eve); half-hearted offering to God (Cain and Abel); pride of wanting to be like God (tower of Babel).

This breakdown, in turn, is always followed by the breakdown in relationship between different people. As soon as God challenges Adam, he responds by blaming Eve for giving him the fruit. He also goes on to blame God for creating Eve in the first place! By blaming Eve, rather than himself, Adam falls out with Eve. Eve, meanwhile, responds by blaming the serpent. We see in Genesis 4 that Cain is envious of Abel, and this leads to the ultimate breakdown of human relationships, when Cain murders his brother. In the Babel story, the breakdown of relationship with God leads to the breakdown of communication between people. Lack of communication leads on to social separation and to the different language groups being scattered and further separated from each other.

We also see the breakdown of our relationships with ourselves. As Adam and Eve gain knowledge, they no longer feel at peace with themselves as they have been created by God, and feel the need for clothes. They break their relationship with God but cannot cope with the guilty feelings that this gives them. Cain's poor relationship with God makes him envious of Abel, and, after the murder of Abel, he cannot face up to the consequences of his own actions. Blaming others and blaming God leads, ultimately, to further separation from other humans and also from God. The breakdown of relationships that we call 'sin' is like a cancerous growth, eating away at all that it touches.

Finally, this breakdown in relationships leads to a breakdown in the relationship between God, humans and creation itself. Not only does Eve fall out with the serpent, so that there is an enmity between her offspring and the serpent's offspring, but from this point onwards the earth produces thorns and thistles and will demand excessive toil from human beings. There will be 'natural' disasters and other disasters, like the consequences of global warming, that are caused by humanity's greed and sinfulness. No longer does creation co-operate with humanity. Creation itself rebels and becomes fallen.

A holistic ministry

While the consequences of these broken relationships are felt in all the families of the earth, God's loving response is to keep taking initiatives to bring restoration. We as the Church are caught up in this task, which includes four different elements.

Personal
The theme running through the whole of the Bible is God's love for the people whom he has created, his constant willingness to offer us new opportunities for restored relationship with him. The prophet Hosea, through his own experiences of having his love rejected, is able to gain a glimpse into the heart of God and begin to understand the depths of his love and forgiveness. Hosea 11:1–3 tells of God's compassion despite Israel's ingratitude:

When Israel was a child, I loved him, and out of Egypt I called my son. The more I called them, the more they went from me; they kept sacrificing to the Baals, and offering incense to idols. Yet it was I who taught Ephraim to walk, I took them in my arms; but they did not know that I healed them.

The events of Jesus' death and resurrection show us the price that God is prepared to pay, and how much he is willing to suffer, in order to reconcile us to him.

As part of being a blessing to the nations, we need to be involved in restoring the relationship between God and individual people. We are the bridges between God and his people that allow the rebuilding of relationship. We need to point to what Jesus did upon the cross and how it is Jesus, the new Adam, who by dying upon a 'tree' undoes the damage that the old Adam caused through his disobedience over a tree in the Garden of Eden. We must proclaim the incarnate, crucified and resurrected Christ as our redeemer, saving each of us individually. The task is not just to proclaim but, as Jesus indicates within the Great Commission in Matthew 28:18–20, to make disciples, baptize and teach everything he has commanded us.

Social and political

We also need to be involved in restoring the broken relationships between people, communities and nations. The early chapters of Genesis end with the breakdown in communication at Babel and the scattering of the peoples. The Holy Spirit heralds the beginning of the Church's mission at Pentecost when we read, in the second chapter of Acts, of the apostles finding themselves understood in different languages. In Matthew 19:19, Jesus says that we must love our neighbours as ourselves. This means that we must address all the evils and injustices that divide people and separate them from each other. We can never be fully in communion with God if we do not try to tackle the issues that separate us from our brothers and sisters, and our brothers and sisters from each other.

Healing

Our task includes both physical and psychological healing. Some Christians will fulfil a healing ministry by undergoing medical training as doctors, nurses or paramedics. A minority of Christians have a spiritual gift of miraculous healing. But healing is more than just responding to physical symptoms. If people do not love themselves, they cannot love their neighbours. The nature of our healing ministry will probably be different from that of Jesus, but we are still called to help within the healing process as people discover that God loves them and accepts them. If people cannot accept and love themselves, then they will, like Adam, project their guilt and disease upon others and upon God.

Environmental

We also need to work to restore the relationship between God, humanity and creation. In Eden, human beings were given stewardship over the animal kingdom and the natural world. Stewardship does not mean exploitation, nor does it mean meeting the wants of one generation at the expense of the needs of a future generation. Politicians are only just beginning to come to terms with the fact that excessive use of fossil fuels, in recent decades, has damaged the ozone layer at the poles and caused 'global warming', which is thought to be influencing climatic conditions. The rainforests of South America and Central Africa moderate the climates of those continents. As they are exploited, this too has a disastrous impact upon climate. Elsewhere the exploitation of the earth's resources has resulted in pollution and poisoning of the environment. Generally with these trends, it is the wealthy who are taking advantage of the planet's resources and the poor who suffer most as a result of the climatic changes. Whilst it is hard to influence the multinational companies and governments who are the main offenders, we can all consider the impact of our own lifestyle.

All four of these elements have been seen as part of our task but, sadly, different groups have often been polarized in their understanding, and have emphasized one aspect to the exclusion of others. This trait is, of course, part of the breakdown of relationships that we see in the fall— a breakdown of communication.

The calling given to the Church is a holistic ministry. It will include all four of these different elements. It is important to remember that, in each of the Genesis stories that we have considered, the first relationship to fracture is that between God and the individual. This implies that our priority must always be the restoration of this relationship because if it is not restored, then whatever else is achieved will probably break down again before too long. It is only when the relationship between people and God is restored that they can truly be in harmony with others, themselves and creation.

It is in the light of this understanding of our task that we turn to specific ministries. The Church has traditionally set aside people to carry out particular duties and has talked in terms of a 'vocation' or calling to these ministries or duties. This does not mean that a vocation may only be to a specific ministry of the Church. People can be called to a task that has not been defined by the Church in such a precise way. Many who are in teaching, medical work, social work or another caring profession will see this as their vocation. Others will see their vocation as simply living out the love of Jesus in an inner city or other challenging setting. Vocation might be voluntary work with young people, the elderly, lonely or the marginalized. Sadly, the downside of creating different, 'professional' Christian ministries is to devalue the Christian work that is not within those ministries.

My first job was within chemical textile research. It was when I conclusively proved that it was far more economical for my employer to continue to throw away its effluents, rather than recycling them, that I started to explore the idea of working with people instead. Perhaps someone should have challenged me at that point as to whether my vocation should have been as a Christian engineer struggling to restore the broken ecological relationship between God, humanity and creation. For many, 'vocation' will be the task of applying Christian values to their everyday work within an environment that has a different set of values. This will often be a tougher and more isolated task than one of the recognized professional Christian ministries.

For many years, CMS used a poster that posed the question, 'Has God called you to stay where you are?' It worked well in stimulating people to consider their calling, and it was also very affirming to many people who could prayerfully answer, 'Yes', and they had not previously been able to consider their current role as a proper vocation. For a good number of people, there is an underlying assumption that a vocation should be for life. We ordain clergy for life, people join religious communities for life and, in days gone by, missionaries went overseas for life, or at least until retirement age. The reality, as far as many modern-day mission partners are concerned, is that receiving churches do not need them for life and that after serving for some years overseas they need to rediscover their Christian calling, perhaps creatively building on their cross-cultural experience whilst working in their home country. For example, having worked with Asians of another faith in Asia, they might be called to work with that same faith and people group within Britain. Having been an outsider in another country, they may do work involving empathy with the outsider in their own country. Their ministry may end up being in a number of different places and perhaps within different countries. And at each phase they need to be exploring what their calling is.

In the same way that it is possible to be both ordained and a mission partner, it is possible to hold together different forms of ministry. The deacon does not cease to become a deacon when ordained priest, and neither role is lost if consecrated bishop. Our ultimate task is obedience to God rather than performing the same role for the rest of our Christian life. The early Church, as we read in Acts 6:1–7, set aside seven people to be deacons, to serve at table, but the Holy Spirit quickly decided that Stephen and Philip had other tasks to perform. Unfortunately, there seems to be an unwritten hierarchy of vocations that exists within people's minds, with full-time Christian employment being seen as the ideal. However, the different tasks of Christian ministry are all part of the body of Christ and all are interdependent upon each other. Paul explains this in 1 Corinthians 12:12–21.

For just as the body is one and has many members, and all the members of the body, though many, are one body, so it is with Christ. For in the one Spirit we were all baptized into one body—Jews or Greeks, slaves or free—and we were all made to drink of one Spirit. Indeed, the body does not consist of one member but of many. If the foot would say, 'Because I am not a hand, I do not belong to the body,' that would not make it any less a part of the body. And if the ear would say, 'Because I am not an eye, I do not belong to the body,' that would not make it any less a part of the body. If the whole body were an eye, where would the hearing be? If the whole body were hearing, where would the sense of smell be? But as it is, God arranged the members in the body, each one of them, as he chose. If all were a single member, where would the body be? As it is, there are many members, yet one body. The eye cannot say to the hand, 'I have no need of you,' nor again the head to the feet, 'I have no need of you.'

We should not forget, either, that our calling does not need to be to a specified ministry. We might be called to live out our lives in the inner cities; we might be called to live and work with those of other faiths within our home town; we might be called to share our faith with our neighbours, to live out a Christian life in the complexities of our workplace, to be reconcilers or to work for justice. It does not need to be a specific ministry, but it is likely that it will fit within the biblical mandate of restoring the personal, social, healing and environmental relationships. It is against this background that we need to be exploring what we feel God might be leading us to. Some people are already aware that they are 'on call', as they feel that they have been put on alert and will soon be asked to prepare for a specific task. But God's work is the responsibility of the whole Church, so the reality is that we are all on call.

CHAPTER 2

'And the Lord said...'

From the earliest Bible stories, we find the idea that God might speak to someone to ask them to do a particular task, or to move to another place. As we read through the Bible, and the lives of different biblical characters, we get a clear picture of a God who communicates with people, time and time again. What is not so clear, however, is exactly *how* God communicates with people. Possibly, those who wrote down the Bible stories did not see this as important. For them, what mattered was the fact that God had communicated, people had responded and things had happened as a result.

Perhaps, words did not always do justice to what these people had experienced. Whatever they had experienced, via whichever of their senses, be it in an instant or over a long period of time, they were sure that God had communicated with them. Usually the writers of the biblical story just concentrated upon the fact that God had communicated, and in so many of these accounts we read, 'The Lord said...'.

Some Christians will readily use such words to describe their own sense of leading. Others will feel that there is a spiritual arrogance in using such language; even so, they will still have a sense that to act in certain ways does tie in with God's will and is a response to what God has done for them and the skills he has given them. However you describe this feeling or thought process, if you are exploring any Christian ministry, it is important that you have some sense that, somehow, God is leading or nudging or communicating with you. You also need to be able to express this in some way.

Through my work with CMS, helping people to explore their vocation for cross-cultural mission, I have been privileged to hear many people share their stories of how they perceived God speaking to them. With the insights that I have gained from such stories, I have looked afresh at the biblical stories and gained some understanding as to how God might have been communicating with people.

A sense of authority

There is no doubt that the first disciples actually heard the voice of God physically, spoken through Jesus, the incarnate Son of God. Their experience of this was unique. While they did not have to agonize over whether or not they had actually heard a voice, they still had to work out who Jesus really was and how they should respond. What can we learn from their experiences? A version of the story of the calling of the first disciples is found in Luke 5:1–11. It is interesting to try to empathize with their feelings as they had this encounter with Jesus.

Have you ever found yourself trying to do something that you are usually good at and, for once, being unable to do it well? Then someone else comes along, who (as far as you know) has no skill at all in the particular activity, and tells you to do it differently! There is probably only one thing worse than that experience, and that is when you do it their way, to show how silly their suggestion was, and you find that they were right.

In Luke 5, we have a group of fishermen. Imagine you are one of them. You are not new to fishing, as it would have been your family's profession for generations, and you would have been involved since you were old enough to climb into a boat. Fishing is one of those occupations where you have good times and bad times. Your knowledge and skill help, but sometimes, no matter what you do, the fish are not there. The night shift is over and, although you have caught nothing, it is time to pack up and have some sleep. You just have to wash the nets first.

Then along comes this carpenter from Nazareth. Nazareth is miles away from the lake and this man does not have a boat of his own, so he asks if you can row him out a little way from the shore to speak to the crowds following him, who seem to think he is some kind of special teacher. The curve of the shore would make a natural amphitheatre.

The carpenter finishes his teaching and the crowd disperses. Your nets have dried in the warmth of the sun and all you need to do is to fold them up before you can go home. It was worth hearing him speak, although you have lost an hour of your sleep and you are very tired by now. But he has not finished with you. He asks you to go out fishing again. This man may be a good carpenter—and he is certainly a good teacher who kept the crowd's attention with his words—but that still doesn't mean that he knows anything about fishing. You point out to him, politely of course, that there are good times to fish and bad times to fish, and this is one of the latter. You, with all your background of living and breathing the trade, could not catch anything. To try further is a waste of time, when you should be in bed sleeping so that you can get out and catch something the next night.

So why do you obey? Is there authority in his voice? Was there authority in his teaching? You obey and find that, immediately, your nets are full.

Who is this carpenter, and teacher, who has such authority? His very presence has shown you your inadequacies and failings. It is not good for you to be with him. His very goodness shows you how sinful you are—but... but he has asked you to join him and told you not to be afraid. He has asked you to catch people rather than fish from now on—whatever that means. Such is his authority that you give up your boat and equipment and the security of your profession, and follow him.

Those first disciples, somehow, recognized an authority in Jesus. Many others heard Jesus speak, and the Holy Spirit caused some to see and recognize and respond to that authority. But it was not just a matter of authority. They recognized that here was someone who could see right through them. They felt that Jesus knew all about them. As in the encounter with the Samaritan woman at the well, recounted in John 4:7–30, Jesus knew and understood their past. Jesus was able to see them not just as they had been and as they now were, but also as they might be. He recognized their potential and encouraged them towards fulfilling that potential.

While we will not meet the incarnate Jesus who speaks with a human voice, we can still meet with the same Jesus in different ways. It might be through his words in the Bible that we read or hear; or through some other writings or words; or within worship, a sermon or our prayer life. As with those first disciples, we suddenly sense that the word or words have been directed, personally, at us. The Holy Spirit illuminates those words for us so that they touch something deep within us, and we feel that we are being spoken to by our Lord.

A personal reflection based upon Luke 5:1–11

This carpenter is still looking for those
who can follow him, to catch people.
He is still looking for those who
can recognize the authority of his teachings;
can respond to the authority of his voice when he speaks to them;
can labour all night and then continue the next day;
are able to put their professional expertise on one side and learn from him;
are able to rely upon his strength rather than just their own;
will do what he says, even if it goes against what others think they should do;
will acknowledge Jesus as Lord;
are aware of their own sinfulness and failings;
can accept Jesus' forgiveness and move on;
are open to learning new ways;
are prepared to leave everything to follow him.

Looking for patterns

We have looked at how Jesus first called some of his disciples, but in Acts 10 one of those disciples, Peter, is aware of the risen and ascended Jesus calling him into a new endeavour and to gain new insights. In this passage, Peter, staying in Joppa with Simon the tanner, is called to go and share the gospel with Cornelius. Cornelius is a

Roman centurion, a Gentile and a 'God-fearer'—that is, not a Jew but someone showing an interest in the God of Judaism.

Reading this story brings back memories of times I spent in Ramallah, ten miles north of Jerusalem, and in Nazareth. I was with groups of young British Christians on the CMS *Encounter* programme, who were sharing for a few weeks in the lives of the local Palestinian Christians. In the morning, we would often be involved in physical work such as painting, building, clearing or planting with our Palestinian counterparts. In the afternoon, after lunch, we would talk with them to find out more about the people, their aspirations, their country, their heritage, the local church situation. But immediately after the morning's work, we would return at midday and head up to the flat roof of our host's house for half an hour before lunch. Like Peter, we would go there intending to pray. Like Peter, after our physical work in the August heat, we would often fall asleep. As well as ourselves, there would be two other things upon the roof—the household washing, including the bed sheets, and aromas from the forthcoming lunch. I always feel that Peter's dream of animals being lowered in sheets, and his desire to eat, was the most natural dream to have in the circumstances!

We will return later to this story and some of its wider implications, but for the moment just look at how God communicates with Peter. Acts 10:3 tells us that it was an angel of God that appeared. Peter's response is, 'What is it, Lord?' When the Lord wants to say something important to Peter, he does it in triplicate. After Jesus was arrested, Peter went through the agony of denying Jesus three times, and had to live with his guilt until that moment at the lakeside, described in John 21:15–17, when Jesus commissioned him three times to his pastoral role as shepherd, with responsibility on earth for Jesus' flock.

Here on the roof-top, Peter again gets a message in triplicate and the penny drops. It is the Lord who is speaking to him. It is not that we should expect God, like a good civil servant, to send his communications to us in triplicate but that we can expect him to speak to us in familiar ways. A valuable exercise, which I have often used at vocational conferences, is to draw a map of our lives and to plot on this the life-changing decisions that we have made. Then we reflect and consider how we perceived God speaking to us as we made these decisions. How did we know that it was God, and not just our own desires? Like Peter, we can expect to find God speaking to us in those same familiar ways in the future.

An ongoing process

As well as seeing sheets drying on the roof, Peter may have been looking out to sea and noticing the sheet-like sails of the boats, as he was staying in the house of Simon the tanner who lived beside the sea. The work of a tanner, involving the skins of dead animals, was ritually unclean and dirty, smelly work. It would not be unusual for someone involved in such work to make their home beside the sea, where they would inconvenience fewer people. Peter was about to be called to share his faith with a Gentile. The vision helps him to prepare to break the Jewish food laws and to offer and receive hospitality with Gentiles, things that good Jews could not do. It is interesting to realize that a good Jew would not visit the house of a tanner, as that would put them in permanent need of ritual cleansing as long as they stayed. With the vision that Peter receives, he is able to cross the barrier of the food laws—and perhaps the fact that he was staying with Simon suggests that he was beginning to move in that direction, anyway. We do not know how or why he was staying with Simon the tanner, but through his vision the Holy Spirit continued the process of transformation.

Peter's vision was no 'Damascus road' experience—but neither do I feel that the original, literal 'Damascus road' experience (the conversion of Paul, recorded in Acts 9) was as sudden and completely unexpected as we assume.

In Acts 7, we read of the stoning of Stephen. One of those present is a young man called Saul. Saul is not directly involved, but has the task of looking after the coats while the others get on with the warm work of a stoning. I wonder what went through Saul's mind as he watched Stephen. As he was being battered to death, this man forgave those who were committing the act. We gain a tremendous image of Stephen, the victim, being calmly and forgivingly in control. Surely his witness must have made a profound impact upon Saul.

Outwardly, it seems to have made Saul even more determined to destroy the Church, but what may have been his inner turmoil as he saw the serenity and love of Stephen and his other victims? Surely that very reaction of hitting out against the Church is a symptom of someone struggling against accepting an unpalatable reality. Saul is struggling with what his head and heart are saying to him. At the head level he cannot accept the claims of Jesus Christ and his followers, but at the heart level he knows that he needs to take them seriously. I am sure that God had already been working away at Saul's understanding long before the encounter on the Damascus road.

So often, what may appear a spontaneous insight is, in reality, the result of a long process that has been going on in our heads. The process may have been going on deep within our hearts and only when we stop and think about it do we realize that the insight is the consequence of awareness that has taken time to develop. This is often the way that God will choose to communicate.

If we look carefully, we can see the same course of events in the story of the calling of Abram in Genesis 12. Abram (or Abraham, as he eventually becomes) is often held up as the best example of a great man of faith, and it is easy to idealize the Abrahamic calling: going off into the unknown, with no knowledge of where we are going but complete faith in the one who calls us onward. Now, the story of Abraham was probably not written down until about a thousand years after it took place. For a thousand years it was passed on orally. Bringing my own perceptions of how people respond to a sense of calling, I began to wonder if some of the verses of the original text had been lost over the years. Why was there no detailed questioning about the proposed location? The modern-day Abram would be expecting a job description, or asking if he could meet some people who had already been sent to this country and who could tell him more about the practicalities.

I was right about verses being missing which shed light upon the call of Abram. But they had not so much been lost as mislaid at the end of the previous chapter. Genesis 11 starts excitingly with the story of the tower of Babel. The last twenty verses are a genealogy that few of us wade through, so that we tend to ignore those important last two verses, Genesis 11:31–32.

Terah took his son Abram and his grandson Lot son of Haran, and his daughter-in-law Sarai, his son Abram's wife, and they went out together from Ur of the Chaldeans to go into the land of Canaan; but when they came to Haran, they settled there. The days of Terah were two hundred and five years; and Terah died in Haran.

It was not Abram who had initiated leaving Ur and setting off for Canaan. It was Terah who had set off with his son Abram and his other dependants. Terah had been living with his family in Ur, which is in modern-day southern Iraq. They set off around what is known as the Fertile Crescent, via Syria, with the intention of going to Canaan. When they reached Haran, in modern-day eastern Syria, they settled there instead. How do we hold this together with the understanding that we gain from chapter 12 that God called Abram out of his homeland to go to Canaan? Did God really call Abram to Canaan? Or did Abram go because his father had decided that the whole family should go there and he was simply carrying out his father's intention?

Recent archaeological research has shown that a lot of migration took place at this time, around the Fertile Crescent from Iraq, via Syria, to Canaan. Terah and his family were part of this migration. What sets Abram apart from the others involved was that he believed that God had called him to move. The missionary movement from Western Europe that began in the 18th century and developed in the 19th century coincided with colonial expansion which brought many from Europe to work in Africa and Asia. The motives for moving varied, but some went overseas because they felt that God had told them to do so.

More recently I have met a number of people whose training has been totally geared to working in a different country—those who have studied Arabic or another language, perhaps a four-year degree course, including a year abroad, followed by a relevant Masters degree; those who have qualifications in tropical agricultural or development studies or who have studied tropical medicine. The first step that they took upon their journey to another country began with applying for a particular college course, without necessarily knowing where it would ultimately take them. In the same way, God did not appear to be directing Abram when his father set off to Haran with him. At a certain point he took stock of his life, and it was maybe at that point that he could see that God had been at work in the decision-making. It is this type of leading, rather than the launch into the great unknown, that is truly in the tradition of Abram.

Let us turn, by contrast, to the story of Jonah. When God calls him, it is not as if he pretends that he has not heard. No; he deliberately sets off in the opposite direction. This reaction is worthy of further exploration.[1] We are introduced to Jonah as the son of Amittai; the same description is given to identify the prophet Jonah mentioned in 2 Kings 14:25. Let us assume for the moment that, given the chronological appearance of the two stories in the Bible, the story in 2 Kings is the earlier one. Surely the fact that Jonah has already been called by God to a prophetic ministry makes his subsequent disobedience even more remarkable? No. In Jonah's case it helps to explain his reaction.

Jonah was originally called to prophesy during the reign of King Jeroboam II of Israel. It was during the reign of Jeroboam II that both Amos and Hosea were active in their ministry, so we have a good idea of what they thought was going on in Israel at the time. Basically, Jeroboam II was a king who did evil and caused Israel to do evil. Usually when Israel did evil, the prophets would point out that it could expect to suffer as a nation. When the nation turned to God it could expect to prosper. The reign of Jeroboam II was an exception to this, however. Israel prospered and its borders were restored to their original positions as territory was recaptured. If Israel had been treated as Israel deserved, then the country's name would have been blotted out from under heaven. God had not given Israel any recent warnings, and felt that he could not blot out Israel in such a way. God was compassionate: he looked upon the suffering of his people and, out of compassion, gave Jeroboam II and Israel success.

The reference in Kings is obscure, but it appears that Jonah was the one who had to explain to Israel what God was doing and not doing, and why. The original audience of the book of Jonah would probably have been familiar with Jonah's role in these other events. Jonah was familiar with a God who could blot out cities and nations if he wished, but who also gave warnings and offered opportunities for repentance before he acted in this way. He was familiar with a God who was compassionate. Jonah's ministry, both in the book of 2 Kings and the book of Jonah, is about the same themes of warnings, destruction, repentance and compassion. The difference is that in 2 Kings he is called to give some good news to his own people and in the book of Jonah he is called to give some bad news to some foreigners.

The phrase, 'Don't shoot me, I'm only the messenger' is tailor-made for Jonah. In 2 Kings, Jonah is called to do something that will make him popular, but in the book of Jonah he will be making himself very unpopular. Jonah appears obedient enough when he has to give good news to his own people, but he runs away from giving the bad news to the foreigners.

The above interpretation is based upon the assumption that the 2 Kings story is the first calling and the book of Jonah the second. If the reverse is true, then we can still see the same themes of warnings, destruction, repentance and compassion being present within both parts of Jonah's ministry.

When we stop and reflect upon what God has been doing within our lives, and the ways in which he has guided and directed us in the past, we begin to see patterns emerging and to see the bigger picture and to make connections. In this way we can begin to see what God is wanting us to do next. Often we will be happy with the prompting that we hear, and rush to embrace it. Sometimes, like Jonah, we will find the consequences rather awesome.

Through whispers and worship

God can speak to us as we make sense of what has been happening in our lives, but how else can we hear him? In 1 Kings 19:11–12, the prophet Elijah finds that God speaks through a still small voice. God asks Elijah to stand on a mountain and experience wind, earthquake and fire, before experiencing silence. It is in the silence, rather than the more dramatic events, that he hears God's voice.

I remember hearing of a candidate with another mission agency (not CMS), who was scheduled to go to a selection conference some years ago. In fact she never got there. The conference had been planned for a December weekend and it snowed so hard that all transport ground to a halt. Accordingly, the conference was postponed a month, until the following January. The January weekend saw more snow but not enough to stop the transport, and the selection went ahead. This particular candidate, however, had met a man shortly before the first conference and became convinced that the snow was sent to stop her going, so that she could marry her new friend and stay in Britain rather than pursue her offer of overseas service. As a result, when it snowed for the second time, she decided not to go to the selection conference after all. Did the other candidates see God at work in their lives in this way? No. They concluded that it is not uncommon to experience snow and difficulties in travelling in December and January, and went ahead to the selection conference.

The trouble with God using bad weather over half the country to make a point to one person is that it is rather inconvenient for everyone else. Those two patches of bad weather caused a number of people to be injured or killed in traffic accidents. Some old people, living by themselves with few resources, died of hypothermia. Many other people had their plans radically changed by that weather, with all types of consequences. Does God really work in this way just to pass on a message to one person?

The prophet Elijah would have expected God to speak through big events. In Old Testament times, God's people were focused within one nation and God often did want to speak to them as a nation, as we have seen in the ministry of Jonah. God would speak through the dramatic events, through national success or disaster. In the New Testament, after the gift of the Holy Spirit is given to the first apostles, it is unusual to read of God speaking through big, dramatic events. As we have seen with Peter and Paul, and will see in the life of other New Testament characters, God is more usually seen speaking to the individual or to the Church. The big, dramatic event might be the stimulus that makes us stop and reflect and allow the Holy Spirit to speak to us. The lady who did not go to the selection conference thought that God had sent the snow for her benefit. The reality was that it brought a pause in the process that allowed her an opportunity to listen to the 'still small voice'. As Elijah found, God can speak to us through the still small voice that follows the wind, earthquake or fire.

Going and standing on a mountain, as Elijah did, is one way of finding the quietness necessary to be able to hear God's whisper. It might mean waiting until after the wind, earthquake and fire have passed, but we will find the quiet there eventually. There will be other ways of finding quiet without climbing mountains. One of the problems of quiet is that we often avoid it because it makes us feel uncomfortable. But God can, and does, speak to us through the quiet, although we do not always want to hear what he is saying to us. We often spend so much time talking to God, telling him what we want and what we think, that we do not have an opportunity to listen to him properly. We miss hearing his whisper to us.

Of course, we can easily mishear the still small voice, and if God has spoken to us alone, then others will not have heard what he was saying. This means that we must not rush ahead on the basis of one still small voice. We need to keep asking God, through our prayers, what he is saying to us. We need to share with others what we feel that God is saying to us and ask them if they feel that this could be true. And we need to ask people who we know will be honest with us, rather than just saying what we want to hear. We will want them to pray for us as we interpret the still small voice, and to see if God confirms with them what we feel that he is saying to us.

Hearing the whisper of God, the still small voice, is just the beginning of trying to understand what God may be saying to us, but it is a better way than expecting to hear him in the earthquake, wind or fire. We may not be able to find an actual mountain to go and listen to what God is saying to us, but just spending a few days quietly at a retreat centre has proved a very valuable way for many people to find the opportunity, within their busy lives, to get in touch with the still small voice of God and hear what he is saying to them.

For Isaiah, the word came from God through a vision. We hear of his calling in Isaiah 6:1: 'In the year that King Uzziah died, I saw the Lord sitting on a throne, high and lofty; and the hem of his robe filled the temple.'

Whether or not Isaiah was at worship when this vision occurred, his vision became an act of worship. Worship should always be an act that lifts us out of our everyday existence and cares, and into the presence of the living God. It should strengthen and inspire us to go back to our daily lives. The realities of our experiences of worship will vary, of course, but in some way or other, at some points in our lives, we have an experience which helps us to understand what Isaiah encounters in this verse.

Isaiah's sense of calling is rooted in an enlarged vision of God and a new appreciation of his awesomeness and majesty. Our vision of God will always be limited and incomplete; but it is often when we see God in a new and different way, when we realize that our understanding of him has been restricted, that we begin to feel called by him. When we are touched afresh by the majesty of God or the love of God, or what God has done for us through Jesus on the cross, we have a deep desire to share that new understanding with others.

Looking for signs

I remember hearing the story of a woman who was praying quietly in church about her future. She was watching the effect of the sun shining through the stained-glass window and could see a patch of red projected upon the wall of the church. The earth's rotation meant that the sun's rays moved on to the adjacent green glass. Suddenly the red light that she had been watching became a green light! She interpreted this as a vocational traffic light: God was giving her the green light to go ahead.

My initial reaction was to dismiss this story. Whether you see a red light or a green light will depend purely upon where you sit within that church, the time of day you are sitting there and whether or not the sun is shining. My reaction now is different. Of course there will be natural explanations as to whether you see a red or a green light, but this begs the question of why you notice and how you interpret that red light changing to green. If we are seeking guidance, and prayerfully waiting on God, then the Holy Spirit will help us. It may not be through a stained-glass window, but through a warm glow or the daily passage of scripture that we are reading, or a word from a friend, or something that simply jumps out at us from the newspaper, television or radio.

Although the story of Gideon, found in Judges 6:36–40, is usually held up as an example of lack of faith, it actually offers very valuable advice about testing what we think that God is saying to us. According to the text, God had clearly already spoken to Gideon. Gideon is asking himself the question that all of us must ask. Is this of God or is it a product of my own desire?

If the sense of calling is just our own desire, then it is quite easy to come up with a 'fleece', a way of testing, that confirms what we want to believe God is saying. To make doubly sure, Gideon gets God to work the test both ways round. On the first night, the fleece is to be covered with dew and the surrounding ground dry. When God has worked this sign, Gideon asks for the fleece to be dry with dew on the ground. It is only when God has confirmed things twice that Gideon is in a position to believe that it really is God speaking to him.

Set aside by the body of Christ

So far, we have focused upon Bible stories in which God has spoken directly to an individual. Often God will speak to others and get them to pass on the message, as was often the task of the Old Testament prophets.

In Acts 6 we have the first example of the Church involved in strategic planning. As the size of the early Church grew, the twelve apostles were feeling the strain of both managing the day-to-day needs of the whole community and spreading the gospel. There were complaints that they were not coping and that the food distribution was not being organized properly. The apostles made a strategic decision. Their priority was to be evangelists rather than managers and servants.

The need to delegate was not a new issue. Moses had been wearing himself out during the exodus, trying to lead the people by himself. We read in Exodus 18 how Moses eventually invited his father-in-law, Jethro, the prototype of the management consultant, to give him helpful advice on delegation.

The Church in Acts consisted not only of local Hebrew Jews but of 'Hellenists', so called because they came from anywhere within the Greek-speaking world. Most would have been Jews by birth, but one of those mentioned in Acts 6:5 is Nicolaus, a proselyte of Antioch. A proselyte was a Gentile who had converted to Judaism. The apostles were Hebrew Jews, and ministering to a mixed group like this raised the problem that if some people became unhappy then differences in language, community and ethnicity would create barriers. The apostles' decision not only eased their own workloads but also solved this problem of the Hellenists complaining about the food distribution.

The apostles did not fall into the trap of deciding themselves whom to choose as deacons. This is the mistake often made by busy people who are used to being in control. I am sure that if the apostles had chosen the seven deacons, the problem would not have gone away. However well balanced the food distribution might have become, there would always have been some people who found fault with it, exploiting the differences within the Christian community as the reason. The apostles, however, not only delegated the task to the Greek-speaking community but they delegated the decision-making process to them as well.

The other common trap related to delegation is to be so keen to get rid of the task that we expect too much of people who have not had to cope with it before. The apostles, surely advised by the Holy Spirit (the ultimate management consultant), avoided this trap as well. They handed over the decision-making so that the people involved chose whom they wanted to serve them, but they also provided clear guidelines for the selectors. In Acts 6:3 we read that the deacons needed to be of good standing, full of the Spirit, and full of wisdom.

The apostles then gave their own affirmation to the whole process (Acts 6:6) by praying over the seven and laying their hands upon them. A task had been delegated within the wider body of the Church, but the decision-making process, and the people chosen, were affirmed by the whole body through this act.

We are given no indication as to whether or not the seven deacons felt any sense of calling themselves. It was the wider Church, using the selection criteria, who prayerfully decided who was right for this particular work. Sometimes the initiative for a calling will come first to the individual, and at other times it will come from the wider body of the Church. Any calling that is truly of God should eventually be confirmed by both the Church and the individual.

Anyone going ahead for some type of Christian ministry will probably have to go through some form of selection process with a representative part of the body of Christ. A familiar New Testament example of this is in Acts 13, when Barnabas and Saul are set aside by the praying community and sent off on their first missionary journey. My experience is that those whose job it is to test vocation are looking for people open to what God is saying to them, rather than someone who appears to have a hotline to heaven. Having said that, it is not right to leave it all to the selection process without seeking awareness of whether or not God is leading us.

It is important that anyone who begins to explore a vocation has some sense that they are being led in that direction and have begun to reflect on how God is speaking to them. They should be open to how others interpret this sense of leading but, at the end of the process, they need a conviction that it is the Lord's leading.

NOTE

1 Before saying anything about the book of Jonah, it is worth commenting upon interpretation. Scholars disagree about the book's dating, and most serious scholars who have engaged in biblical criticism do not connect Jonah with the prophet identified as Jonah son of Amittai, referred to in a brief and obscure reference in 2 Kings 14:25. However, a more recent approach is a literary study of the narrative within the Old Testament. This method is described in detail in *Narrative in the Hebrew Bible* by David M. Gunn and Danna Nolan Fewell, Oxford University Press, 1993. Within this approach you try to understand what would have been communicated to the original hearer of the story through the narrative techniques used by the teller of the story. To do this, you do not start off with a 21st-century worldview, but with the worldview of those who first heard the story. Their worldview would have been based upon the Hebrew scriptures of the time—the books of Genesis to 2 Kings inclusive. My assumption, using their methodology, is that the original hearers would have immediately identified the book of Jonah with the prophet mentioned in 2 Kings 14:25. Using this approach, we can assume that the book of Jonah is about this same Jonah being called by God, for a second time, to act as a prophet.

CHAPTER 3

Wrestling with God

As we begin to reflect upon the fact that God does still call people for his work in this day and age, the following meditation, taking Genesis 27 as its starting point and also relying upon Isaiah 45:1, might be helpful.

Lord, it is not fair.
Why did you choose Jacob rather than Esau?
Esau was the good and obedient son, pleasing his father.
Jacob was sly and a trickster.
Taking advantage of his brother's hunger, he stole his birthright.
Plotting with his mother, he obtained the blessing that was meant for Esau.
While Esau was obediently hunting for game, Jacob was idling while his mother worked for him.
While Esau was obediently hunting for game, Jacob was taking your name in vain.
He explained that it was you who had given him success when it was really his own deviousness.
Jacob lied in order to get the blessing that was meant for Esau.

Lord, it is so unjust—
The way in which you use sinners and not just good people.
When Judah was exiled in Babylon, why did you not use your people to end their own exile?
Instead you used proud Cyrus, the Persian, to defeat the Babylonians and allow Judah to return home.
Time and again, Lord, you use the sinful people rather than the good people.
You use their failings to help you in your purposes.
You bring good out of their weaknesses.

Lord, it worries me that you work in this way.
Like Jacob, I am a schemer who can take advantage
of the weaknesses of others.
I am a liar and an idler.
Like Cyrus, I am proud and can trample over others.
I am a sinful person.
Lord, it worries me.
It is not so much how sinful I am, but that you might use me.
Could my failings be used for your purposes?
Could you bring good out of my weaknesses?

Lord, it concerns me that you call people who are sinful.
It concerns me that you call people because you have tasks
they can fulfil for you.
Lord, it worries me that you call people for responsibilities
rather than for privilege.
Lord, it worries me that you might call even me.
Go away from me, Lord, for I am a sinful man.
Lord, it is not fair.

Our unworthiness

If we are beginning to sense that God might be wishing to use us in a specific way, how do we respond? Gideon, whom we considered in the last chapter, starts off in Judges 6:13 being quite cynical in his response. He wants to know why God has let matters get into such a sorry state. When the Lord explains that he is with Israel, and will help them throw off the oppression of the Midianites, Gideon points out that if the Lord was really with Israel, then they would not have got themselves into such a mess in the first place! Having got this little outburst out of his system, he then focuses upon his own inadequacies. Gideon is the least important son in a family of the weakest clan. Who is going to listen to him? A sense of cynicism, or of our own inadequacy, are both common responses to a calling from God. A sense of our sinfulness is another response.

The Bible tells us stories of a whole range of responses to God's call. Many of those who are called plead with God, begging him to change his mind. Jonah, as we have already mentioned, doesn't even bother to plead, but just sets off in the opposite direction. A modern-day version of Jonah's approach is for people to apply for other jobs instead of following God's lead. If these applications are unsuccessful, they have been better able to see what God really wanted them to do. It is their equivalent of Jonah's flight from port to ship, ship to whale, and whale to dry land! Of course, the natural response to any sense of calling is likely to include a sense of questioning. It is important to remember, though, the lesson that Israel so often forgot: we are not called for privilege but for responsibility. We are not called because we are perfect and sinless, but because God can still use us in our fallen state.

We have looked at how Isaiah received his sense of call in response to perceiving the greatness of God in a new way, and what happened first is that he realized his own sinfulness and unworthiness. In Isaiah 6:5, we read, 'Woe is me! I am lost, for I am a man of unclean lips, and I live among a people of unclean lips.'

Isaiah feels that he is unworthy even to see the vision, let alone respond to it. Unworthiness can be difficult to cope with. Do we really feel forgiven? If we lack a real sense of God's forgiveness, we can mistake a desire to put things right with God for a sense of calling.

Sometimes, when people are converted later in life, they feel an immediate, powerful urge to become either a priest or a missionary! Sometimes this is a true response to a calling, but sometimes it is the result of not really understanding and experiencing God's forgiveness. God forgives our sins but that does not take away their consequences. We still need to live with the consequences of our sins, and what we think is a calling may in fact be an attempt to pay for the consequences of sin. The inner reasoning goes, 'My sins are so bad that I cannot be fully forgiven by God. I can try to put this right with him by sacrificing my life to his service'; or, 'Although I am now a Christian, my past sins have caused certain things to happen which have damaged other people's lives. I cannot put this right with them but I can try to put it right with God by sacrificing my life to his service.'

A sense of guilt is very different from a calling. If we respond out of guilt, we are going to work for God not out of love either for him or for the people that we will be serving, but for selfish motives. If we do not have an experience of God's forgiveness and of his love for us, we will always be limited in what we are able to share with others.

The story of Isaiah's call goes on to include finding true forgiveness: 'Then one of the seraphs flew to me, holding a live coal that had been taken from the altar with a pair of tongs. The seraph touched my mouth with it and said: "Now that this has touched your lips, your guilt has departed and your sin is blotted out"' (Isaiah 6:6–7).

The imagery of this vision gives a clear insight into Isaiah's sense of the sin being blotted out and forgiven. His sin was that of unclean lips. This is not just the ritual impurity of, for example, breaking the food laws, but an impurity of lifestyle through being contaminated by his involvement with an arrogant, dishonest, decadent people. Symbolically, it is Isaiah's lips that are cleansed. It is only when we have the same sense of God's forgiveness that we can echo the prophet's words in Isaiah 6:8: 'Here am I; send me!'

Our ability to receive

Calling may come from a sense of receiving God's forgiveness, but other giving and receiving may also be involved. Jesus makes this clear in Mark 10:29–30:

Jesus said, 'Truly I tell you, there is no one who has left house or brothers or sisters or mother or father or children or fields, for my sake and for the sake of the good news, who will not receive a hundredfold now in this age—houses, brothers and sisters, mothers and children, and fields, with persecutions—and in the age to come eternal life.'

In verse 28, Peter has been mentioning the cost of following Jesus. Jesus replies by listing what does need to be given up, but he also states that these losses will be repaid a hundred times in this present age.

The costs are real, and need to be understood if the repayment is to be fully understood. Although Jesus was speaking to people within a different culture and time, his words easily translate to our world today. 'Houses' represent our security, both financial security and the sense of belonging to an area and to a church. 'Brothers and sisters' are our immediate and extended families—the joy of seeing nephews and nieces growing up, for example. 'Mothers and fathers' gave us the support that we needed when we were young and might need our support in years to come. They may be parents who do not really understand what we are doing and why, or the parent for whom we cannot be available in their final days. 'Children' face risks to their health, education and their ability to relate to their own culture and peer group, while we long to protect and do our best for them. 'Land' represents our livelihood, our language, our culture and identity.

Luke's version of this story mentions giving up wives as well. Both CMS and I feel that the modern-day understanding of a Christian marriage demands that any response to calling must be entered into equally by both partners in a marriage. That is why I turn to the version in Mark rather than Luke!

Following Jesus does involve sacrifices, very real sacrifices, and we must not make light of the giving that is involved. Jesus promises eternal life in the world to come, but also speaks of the repayment that will come in this present life. Those who give will be repaid a hundred times over. Will the repayment be in a supernatural way? Like manna from heaven? Hardly—Jesus is talking about receiving in the same form as the sacrifices that were made. We will receive from those we go to serve and we will receive from them far more than we have given up. In Romans 16:3–11, Paul sends his greetings to those who have helped him whilst he has been ministering to them. He speaks of Rufus' mother as being like a mother to him and refers to others as kinsmen or relatives. Paul obviously found that the relationships that he had given up to pursue his calling were repaid within new relationships.

A friend, Katie, tells a powerful story of some time that she spent working with the dying in Calcutta. She befriended an elderly lady who owned virtually nothing. Shortly before she died, the lady wanted to give Katie a mango. It was the only mango the lady had, and Katie had money to buy her own mangoes. Katie tried to refuse but the lady was persistent. Katie eventually accepted the mango and also accepted the fact that her previous refusal had been a statement that she had nothing to receive from this lady. Her acceptance was a sign of their common humanity and gave a final dignity to a person dying an undignified death.

Whether or not we are privileged to receive in this way will depend upon whether or not we have the capacity to receive. If we see ourselves as the privileged, the bountiful and always the giver, then this restricts our capacity to receive. I can recall numerous occasions, in this country as well as abroad, when I have been the recipient of overwhelming generosity and hospitality from those who could least afford it. It has been a very humbling experience. It has made me feel ill at ease and vulnerable. I have wanted to give to God through my service to others, but I have wanted to give to God on my terms rather than on God's terms. His way has broken down the barriers of class, colour, background, wealth and history, and led to true fellowship and friendship. If we are not able to receive graciously from our brothers and sisters in Christ, then how can we receive God's grace in all its fullness? God can only send those who have the capacity to receive.

Prior expectations

Some people are not surprised at all by a sense that God might be setting them aside for a specific task. They are brought up within a family or a church that sees it as perfectly natural, and they have an expectation that they will be called to a particular form of ministry or mission. Being called in some way can be seen as the family business.

In Old Testament times, being a priest was a family business. You could only become a priest if you were of the house of Levi. Samuel was not of the house of Levi, however. In 1 Samuel 1—3, we read how his mother, Hannah, made a deal with God. If God would give Hannah a son, she would give that son to God's service. When she does have a son, Samuel is given to Eli, the priest, so that Eli can bring him up to serve God, and Hannah is blessed with further children. In Britain in years gone by, it was common practice in some families for one of the sons to be dedicated to the Lord and marked out for priesthood. The first son would inherit the family estate, but what should become of the other sons? Careers within the Army or the Church could solve the dilemma.

Nowadays a vocation is not seen as something to be passed on through a family by right. There can be very strong expectations within some families, however, that the children will have a vocation. This is particularly true when others in the family have had such a calling. There can be a feeling, whether real or imagined, that the family expects you to go into some type of full-time Christian ministry. Failure to do so will be a failure to live up to their expectations. Not having such a calling might, in some way, be seen as not loving God as much as the others do. At another level, because of their up-bringing, people in such families do have a deeper understanding of the realities of the vocation. They know about the family pressures and pains and sorrows as well as the joys and fulfilment, and when, deep down, they are afraid of letting down the family or letting down God, they can find it confusing to hear clearly what God is really saying.

Given the fact that Samuel had been dedicated to God to be used, and had the expectation of priesthood put upon him by his mother, it is interesting to read, in chapter 3, how he discerns for himself the call to become a prophet. Samuel hears a voice calling his name in the night. He assumes that it is Eli. He goes and approaches Eli, who tells him to go back to bed. This happens three times before Eli suggests that the voice might be the Lord's.

Perhaps I am reading too much into the text, but I find it interesting that this person, who is called against a background of expectation that he will have some kind of ministry, has to have the call repeated so often. If you feel particular expectations upon you about a vocation, then I suggest that you do what Samuel did. First of all, go and talk to someone who is not related to you: talking to your priest or pastor can be a good starting point. Keep listening and keep asking others.

As far as overseas service is concerned, someone else who may have an expectation of a calling is someone who has already served overseas and has needed to return to their home country, perhaps for family reasons. Sometimes they return to their home country making a commitment to go overseas again when circumstances allow. If returning overseas becomes possible later on, they should carefully explore whether or not it is God's plan for them at that time, rather than simply fulfilling a promise that has been made in the past.

Known by God

One question with which we may grapple, as we begin to sense God's leading, is to what extent we are free agents. Has God got it all worked out anyway? We read in Jeremiah 1:4:

> *Now the word of the Lord came to me saying,*
> *'Before I formed you in the womb I knew you,*
> *and before you were born I consecrated you;*
> *I appointed you a prophet to the nations.'*

Does this mean that God has our whole life mapped out? Before any of us are born, has he decided who will become Christians, who will be called to specific tasks of mission, and when and what they will be called to? If we accept this, we end up with a creator who starts his creation like a clockwork train set and then watches while every piece moves as planned. If God is so completely in control, can anyone involved in discerning a call ever come to a wrong conclusion? If someone does gets it wrong and doesn't move as they should do, what happens? If fallible people like me are responsible for helping to test calling, when God has it all worked out, then what happens when I make a mistake? Returning to the clockwork train set analogy, those, like me, who operate the signals and the points will end up accidentally putting some of the trains into life's sidings and even being responsible for a few derailments.

If the future is totally mapped out, we lose the concept of free will and end up with a fatalistic approach to life. If the future is mapped out, God becomes a rather bored observer who knows exactly what will happen next, rather than a participant who enters into our lives and suffers with us in our failings and rejoices with us when we get it right.

But does the passage in Jeremiah actually say that God knows what will happen, or does it say that God knows us? Hebrew, like the French language, has two distinct meanings of the verb 'to know'. One meaning, like the French verb *savoir*, is about information, while the other, like the French verb *connaitre*, is about relationship. The passage does not say that God knows exactly what we will do even before our birth, but that he knows us as people. God has the intimacy of relationship with us at all stages of our lives, whether we feel that intimacy ourselves or not.

Psalm 139 also speaks of God knowing us from the womb and through the different stages of our lives. The Wild Goose Worship Group song 'Here am I' is based upon Psalm 139 and develops the theme of God meeting us at different times within our lives. In one verse it says:

> *In the tensions of youth I met you,*
> *Whether shy or uncouth,*
> *Always searching for the truth.*

This reminds us that God is there, meeting with us not only in the parts of our lives that we are proud of, but also in the parts that we would rather forget!

If I am to explore what God is saying to me at a particular point in time, I need to explore where he has been in my life until now. Where was he in those dark episodes of my life? According to both Jeremiah and Psalm 139, he was with me. If God appeared distant at those times, was it because I was shutting him out of my life, and if so, why? If I am carrying hurts and pains in parts of my life which, for whatever reason, I am trying to keep away from God, then I will need to tackle them. I will need to seek healing within my home community and culture rather than taking this pain into the unknown where I might not be able to cope with the consequences. Parts of my life may need prayer; other parts may need professional counselling or psychiatric help. Acknowledging that we need help is not a sign of weakness, or a sign that we are not appropriate for God to use in his mission. Rather it is a sign of self-knowledge and the beginning of the healing process. God has known us as individuals since we were in our mother's womb. He knows the inner secrets of our lives and still loves us. He wants us to know ourselves fully and to love ourselves. That is why he might say to us those words he said to Jeremiah: 'Before I formed you in the womb I knew you, and before you were born I consecrated you; I appointed you a prophet to the nations' (Jeremiah 1:5).

Self-doubt

The book of Jeremiah is not an easy one to read and understand. What emerges from it is not just the actions and the writings of the prophet, but also deep insight into his feelings. We hear how he tried to understand not only what he felt God was saying to him but also the action and inaction of God. Jeremiah comes across as far more vulnerable and sensitive than any of the other prophets. Time and time again, God tells him to speak, and he speaks and people ignore him and despise him. He waits for the coming disaster that he has foretold and nothing happens. Jeremiah is left to wrestle with the question of whether God had told him to speak or whether it was simply his own imagination.

It was not as if Jeremiah was an outward-going, confident extrovert in the first place. When God calls him to prophesy, it is the last thing that he wants to do. He explains to God (Jeremiah 1:6) that he is too young and does not know what to say, but God assures him that he, God, will speak through Jeremiah.

Jeremiah's ministry, which spanned forty years—from his call in the thirteenth year of King Josiah (626BC) until the fall of Jerusalem in 587BC—is finally vindicated after Judah is taken into exile in Babylon. Jeremiah was not the only prophet of his generation; there were plenty of false prophets, prepared to make pronouncements that were far more popular than Jeremiah's woeful message. More than most, Jeremiah had to wrestle with the question that confronts all who go into Christian ministry at some point: 'Does God really want me to be here doing this or did I imagine it all?'

'Now the word of the Lord came to me saying…' (Jeremiah 1:4). What does it mean to have the 'word of the Lord' come to you? How do you know that it is the word of the Lord? Jeremiah was obviously someone who thought deeply and reflected on issues. Was he hearing the word of the Lord or was he acting on the result of processing the available information?

To be sure that they are acting in response to God, Christians today should explore their sense of calling prayerfully, with other Christians, at every stage before seeking to have it confirmed by the appropriate representatives of the Church. If you have family, you need to be convinced that the process has taken into account all members of your family. What will it mean for your children? What will they need to give up so that you can fulfil your sense of vocation? What are the expectations of your own parents? Who is going to meet their needs? Have everyone's expectations and aspirations been realistically explored? You need to be sure that the process has explored your weaknesses and your vulnerabilities as well as your strengths and gifts, taking into account the choice of location and work.

Many people find that attending a vocational conference is a helpful way to start exploring a calling. They can meet people there who are used to helping others to discern their calling, and they can talk with others who are also exploring their own future. You can find further information about such day and residential events in the Appendix (pages 142–143).

Wrestling with God

Uncertainties do not only surface at the beginning of the process. They can come at any point and at any time. Before I joined CMS, I had always been bewildered by the events described in Acts 16:6–10. I could never understand how Paul was restricted from going into Asia. After coming across CMS mission partners who needed to change their intended locations, the thought crossed my mind that perhaps Paul had been refused his visa for Asia! A more likely interpretation, though, is that Paul had health problems. Given that the text changes its focus from 'Paul and his companions' to 'we' at this point, it suggests that the author of Acts, Luke the physician, had just arrived. Possibly Paul was struggling with the 'thorn in the flesh' that he refers to in 2 Corinthians 12:7, and Doctor Luke ordered a change of location!

Whatever the reason, these verses have cheered those who, in later centuries, would not get their visas or their medical clearance for where they expected to go. When I started to write this, two countries were foremost in my mind—one in central Africa and one in central Asia—where, for different reasons, all mission personnel had been evacuated in the previous month. The experience of being prevented from going to or staying in the country that you feel called to is almost always painful, difficult and confusing. Sometimes it can lead to a questioning of the whole sense of call.

The passage in Acts 16 can reassure us in two ways. Firstly, if we experience such an upheaval, we are in good company because it happened to Paul. If someone as close to the Lord as Paul can get it wrong, and find that they have really been called somewhere else, then we should not be overwhelmed if it happens to us. Secondly, we should be reassured by the thought that God still had a plan for Paul. In Acts 16:9, Paul sees a vision of a Macedonian asking him to go to Macedonia to help them. God had to close one door to show him that a different one, to a different place, was opening.

Over the years, I have known a number of people who have had this experience of doors closing. It has never been easy at the time but, with hindsight, they have been able to see God working to bring good out of the confusion and helping them to learn and grow, and draw closer to him, through the experience.

I remember two young people exploring two years' service with CMS. He was bound for Africa and she was heading off to Asia. They met at a selection conference and fell in love during their training. Due to a diplomatic incident, the African country stopped issuing visas to British subjects. The next most likely location for him was the Asian country where she was going. Somehow God had ensured that they were in the same country, but coping with being engaged is not easy when you are several hundred miles apart and living in a culture where you are not expected to be alone together when you do meet. An incident in that Asian country led to the introduction of fixed-term visas and they both had to leave after six months. Eighteen months later, after marriage and further training, they were serving long-term in Africa, in the location where he had originally been bound. Neither of them felt that God had engineered the international incidents in Africa or Asia for their benefit, but they did feel that God could bring good for individuals out of such events.

Paul lived in a world where, because he was a Roman citizen, he could cross frontiers and enter different countries quite freely. Nowadays, with the exception of reciprocal arrangements such as exist within the European Union, a visa, work permit or residence permit is needed to enter any country and stay there legally. International events often mean that people do need to leave countries, temporarily at least. Being called to go to another country means being called to live with uncertainty and being open to finding that plans have to change. If you are too devastated by finding that one door has closed, you may not be open to the Spirit leading you to another location, bringing good in the midst of pain, chaos and confusion.

Wrestling with God

If you are beginning to explore a possible calling to ministry, like Jacob in Genesis 32:22–32, you will have begun to wrestle with God. The Bible passage is ambiguous concerning the identity of the person with whom Jacob is wrestling. In verses 24, 25 and 28 it is a man, but in verse 30 Jacob declares that it was God who had been his adversary. We, too, will face the same ambiguity. The issues with which we wrestle will often seem human enough but, at a deeper level, we will have been wrestling with God.

Jacob wrestles and refuses to let go. Once we realize that we are caught up in a wrestling match, we can let go, abandon the wrestling match and keep God at a distance. But if we feel that we are truly being called, we must continue to wrestle through the night like Jacob. And if we wrestle with God, we must be prepared, like Jacob, to be blessed but also to be injured. Jacob had his hip dislocated and was left limping and incapacitated. We must be open to the same experiences.

We begin to explore a sense of calling to particular work but are eventually told, by selectors, that this is not what God wants us to do. The decision may hinge upon some truth, some partial truth and (given that selectors are human) some misconceptions. The process is often painful and confusing and we may well be left limping away from the encounter.

We give up a good job to go and serve God overseas but the work permit or visa fails to come through and we cannot go; serving in another country either puts pressure upon our family out there, or we find we cannot give support to family at home when it is needed; after years of faithful service, our presence in another country is the obstacle that stops a local person from taking over work that they are perfectly able to do. Our presence is resented and it is time to return.

Such experiences will involve us in wrestling with God, with the risk of injury as well as blessing. A dislocated joint is painful but we have a choice of either living with the pain or risking a short burst of more intense pain to have the joint restored, so that we can move onwards and away from the pain. The same is true of the con-sequences of wrestling with God. We can live with our pain and even show off our limp to others, or we can tackle the source of the pain and seek healing so that we can move forward again without the limp.

Dare we ask *who* has hurt us? Has the encounter been with a person or with God? At one level it was with a person but at a deeper level, like Jacob, we have been wrestling with God. The pain is even less bearable when it is God, rather than people, who has left us hurt and limping. We will feel that it was not fallen humanity that hurt us, but the God who we thought loved us, the God whom we were trying to serve as a token of our love for him. How could such a God hurt us?

We do need to be prepared to ask this question, otherwise we can so easily project the causes of our hurt on to others. At times, God will hurt us to save us greater hurt at a later stage. We might be left limping to stop us from rushing headlong into some situation that would have given us even more pain later on. We may have been hurt when our sense of calling was not affirmed, to save us from the deeper hurt that we would have suffered in entering a situation without the resources to cope.

This does not fully answer the question of why we needed to be hurt at all. The rest of the answer lies in remembering the character of Jacob. We are not called because we are perfect. Like Jacob, we are called because God has a task for us despite our weaknesses and failings. If we were perfect, then we could walk hand in hand with God, always aware of what he is saying, and what he wants from us, and there would be no need for the wrestling and the pain. If we can identify our shortcomings rather than projecting the source of our hurt on to others, we can, with God's help, begin to address our failings. God does not want us to be hurt; he wants his Holy Spirit to work within us to make us perfect, so that we can walk hand in hand with him and know his will for our lives. Wrestling with God is not only about being left limping. Jacob leaves not only with an injury but with the new name of Israel, meaning 'the one who strives'. God acknowledged Jacob's tenacity and endurance and Jacob was blessed by God: he knew that God's purposes would be fulfilled in some way through him. We too may be hurt, but by tackling that hurt we can be assured of God's blessing when we wrestle with God.

CHAPTER 4

Growth

Using your talents

I recently heard a retelling of a familiar parable.

*A father was going away on a long trip to a distant land. He called his
two sons to him and gave them each a thousand pounds.*

*Six months later the father returned and called his older son to him.
The son said, 'Father, you entrusted me with one thousand pounds. Here,
see, I have gained another thousand.' The father replied, 'Well done, my
good and faithful son, I will put you in charge of many things. Come,
share your father's happiness.'*

*He then called his younger son to him. The younger son said, 'Father,
you entrusted me with one thousand pounds. I lost it all to my brother
playing cards!'*

The talents spoken of in Jesus' parable in Matthew 25:14–30 were a
unit of currency: a talent of silver in Israel weighed about 100 pounds
(45 kg) and a talent of gold weighed about 200 pounds (91 kg). I do
not know the derivation of our modern usage of 'talent' to mean skill
or ability, but I feel that Jesus was using a reference to money as an
analogy for skills. I do not know the motivation of the person who
reworked this parable, but it reminds me of certain economic truths
that apply to money, but not to skills:

- Within a closed economic system, there is only a certain amount of
  wealth.
- If someone is to gain money, then it will be at the expense of
  someone else losing money.

- If you are looking for a high rate of return on an investment, then the risks will be high.
- Investing is a form of gambling: there may be some skill involved but there is a lot of luck.

I feel that the original parable is about how we use our skills and abilities for the Kingdom rather than how we use our money for the Kingdom.

As I read Matthew 25:14–30 again, I am keen to know why the three servants behave in the way they do. The Bible is very good at telling us the facts of a story but rarely gives pointers to why people behave as they do. Perhaps one of the features of any parable is that the hearer needs to work at the story in the light of their own experiences. In doing so, they are left with answers that can help in their personal circumstances.

The traditional understanding of this parable is that the master had a good idea of how his servants would perform, and gave out the talents accordingly. The fact that the five-talent servant gains another five, the two-talent servant only gains another two and the one-talent servant gains nothing is a vindication of the original distribution. My own experience of people and of human nature suggests a different interpretation. I do not believe that they were given different numbers of talents because the master knew how they would perform, but I believe that they behaved differently because of the number of talents they were given. The resources that they were given determined their behaviour!

God has given us all different talents—the skills and abilities that we have—to use for his Kingdom. The distribution of these talents has not been equal, but no one starts without any at all. The 'five-talent' people are those who are very aware of their own special abilities, which they confidently use for the Kingdom. The 'two-talent' people do not think that they have amazing skills to share but know that they have something and get on with using these skills. The 'one-talent' people do have some ability, but they look around at those with more and decide to bury what they have rather than using it for the good of the Kingdom.

This interpretation of the parable presents us with both bad news and good news. The bad news is that if we do not use our God-given talents, and choose to bury them, they will ultimately be taken away from us. The good news is that when we do use our skills, they can improve like the best of financial investments. When people use their abilities for the Kingdom, they often find that those abilities grow. In sharing your faith with others, you learn how to do so more sensitively and effectively. By leading Bible studies and discussion groups, you begin to develop your leadership and enabling skills. You need to try public speaking or writing in order to develop the necessary skills further. I have been very fortunate to see people growing their talents over the years, including those whom I interviewed years ago, who were not at all confident that they had much to offer God. They offered what they did have and over the years they have grown both in confidence and in the skills and abilities that they can offer to God.

God has given us all different talents but he has not decided how we will use them for the Kingdom. That is for us to decide. And we are called not only to use our own talents as best we can for the Kingdom, but also to encourage others to use their talents better. Human nature being what it is, somebody with fewer talents is less likely to use them when there are people present with more skills. If you have more talents than others, it is your God-given duty to help those with fewer to use and develop what they have.

The parable also reminds us that we should be humble in our use of our talents. They are not ours by right, but are lent to us by God to use for his work. Any praise that the talents earn must be directed to the master who gave us charge of them, and not to us as the humble servants who use them.

If our skills and abilities need to be grown, we need to remember that growth takes time. It follows that any vocation, using such skills and abilities, will also need to grow over a period of time. This goes against much modern Western thinking. In his book *The Good Shepherd*,[1] the late Lesslie Newbigin explored our culture's increasing interest in the gifts of the Spirit and the lack of interest in the fruit of the Spirit. He argued that this was the result of the move from a rural to an industrial society. A rural society understands all about the need for growth—that it takes time and that, often, much of it is not visible to the eye. An industrial society has no such understanding and can only make sense of what seems instant. If this explains attitudes to the gifts and fruit of the Spirit, I feel that it also often affects attitudes to vocation. When we begin to gain a sense of vocation, we usually need to nurture it. I interviewed someone recently who spoke about his first sense of calling to the Church Army, thirty years ago. His vicar told him to come back in a year's time and let him know if he still had that sense of calling. If his vocation was real, it would continue to grow; if it was not of God, it would wither and fade. The growth of his sense of vocation during that year was a great encouragement to him. We have to look not only at what we have to offer but also at what we still need to develop. It is worth thinking through, at an early stage, what some of your own development and training needs might be, and beginning to discuss with others how these might be addressed.

Nowadays much emphasis is placed upon professional development. Younger people have to bear in mind whether a particular job or life experience will tie in with their future profession. It is easy for an older generation, brought up with ideas of sacrifice, to see this as an unspiritual approach. Wherever God is leading us in the longer term, it makes sense for us to gain appropriate skills in the shorter term to enable that longer-term vocation. In exploring vocation, it is important to check whether the potential next stage in life is likely to lead you closer to what you feel God wants you to do in the future, or whether it is likely to lead you into a cul-de-sac. Vocational development and professional development may not be so different from each other, after all!

Short-term experience programmes

He was an eloquent, articulate, learned young man from a big university city. His family were all believers and he had been brought up within the Christian faith with a thorough knowledge of the scriptures. He had been instructed in the way of the Lord and he spoke with great fervour and taught accurately about Jesus.

After finishing at the university, as a result of his great fervour he felt called to go and share his knowledge of Jesus with one of the new, younger churches—a church in another country that did not have the advantage of being steeped in an understanding of God that went back hundreds of years, whose people did not have the same level of education that he had. The local Christian leaders in the other country heard him speak, with all his confidence and knowledge of the scriptures, and they realized that in fact his understanding of Christianity was to some extent inadequate. They invited him into their homes and helped him to a full understanding of the gospel.

This is actually the story of Apollos, found in Acts 18:24–28, but it might just as easily be the story of any one of thousands of young Christians who go out on short-term programmes. Verse 25 tells us about Apollos, 'He spoke with burning enthusiasm and taught accurately the things concerning Jesus, though he knew only the baptism of John.' Apollos would have seen the need for repentance and recognized Jesus as the Messiah, and would have realized the task of evangelism that Jesus gives to all his followers. He would have had a head knowledge of Christianity but would have lacked a real experience of Jesus working in his life through the Holy Spirit. For all of us, our Christian pilgrimage should be an experience of discovery, and of moving on into full spiritual maturity. An inadequate understanding of Christianity can result from a lack of a real experience to back up our head knowledge. If we have been brought up within the faith and within a particular culture, then we, like Apollos, will know what answers our faith gives to the everyday questions that we encounter, but we will not have had to work through what our faith means for ourselves. When we take our faith into a new culture, we need to ask ourselves new questions and begin relating our faith not just to knowledge but also to our new experience. This can be a confusing time but if we are fortunate, like Apollos, we can find local Christians to help us to understand our faith fully.

So what became of Apollos? When it was time for him to leave (Acts 18:27), the local Christian leaders encouraged him in his ministry. They wrote to other church leaders, telling them to welcome him and to use him as a teacher. We do not know whether or not he went on to have much more cross-cultural experience of mission. No one knows for certain who was the author of the letter to the Hebrews, but one of those on the list of possibilities is Apollos. Hebrews is the letter that engages most deeply with relating the good news of Jesus to the Hebrew understanding. Many of those who have served outside their own culture have gained, on return, new insights into their own culture. I have no proof, but I like to think that it was the short-term experience of Christianity within another culture that enabled Apollos to write the letter to the Hebrews.

Apollos was the prototype of the 'short-termer', a word generally used to refer to those going on cross-cultural mission programmes for a period of less than two years (details of CMS's short-term programmes are given in the Appendix on pages 139–140). Such programmes can help somebody to discover how they cope with the overall experience, both the uncertainty and the opportunity for personal and spiritual growth. It can help the sending agency to see whether the individual is open to learn from contact with national Christians in another culture. If they are not open to such learning, it is unlikely that they are being called to any long-term service overseas!

The short-term experience is a very popular way of testing calling, but the Bible gives us other examples of how people have been encouraged to learn and grow. We have much to learn from their examples.

Learning on the job

In Acts 8:26–39, we read about the encounter between Philip and the Ethiopian official. The term 'Ethiopia' referred to black Africa and would not have been restricted to modern-day Ethiopia. This black African was reading from the book of Isaiah. The assumption is that he was probably reading one of what we refer to as the Servant Songs and that Philip gave him the traditional Christian interpretation that the suffering servant was, in fact, a reference to Jesus. But where did this traditional Christian understanding come from? When was it formulated? It is possible that it had been developed by the time of this encounter, but it is unlikely as the events recounted in this story happened very early in the life of the Church, during a time of both rapid expansion and persecution, long before even the first Gospel was written. Is it not far more likely that it was Philip himself who made the connection, there and then? This insight was a result not of theological research but in response to the question of the black African official. As he shared his faith, Philip had to face questions that he had not previously considered and, guided by the Holy Spirit, his own understanding grew.

Interestingly, I have come across this phenomenon in the lives of modern-day Christians. As they have engaged deeply with poverty, suffering and those of other faiths, they have been asked questions for which their biblical training has not prepared them. In attempting to answer such questions, their own Christian understanding has increased and led to them to new, unexpected insights.

Learning about ourselves

Someone else who did some travelling, with the consequence of gaining experience, was Jonah. In fact, he did a lot more travelling than he was meant to! When Jonah finally gets to Nineveh, we understand why he is so reluctant. It is not because he does not feel that he has the ability, as God has already shown him, on the boat, that he can work through Jonah's words. The problem is that Jonah prefers to believe in a God who condemns and punishes those who are different, rather than a God who wants people to repent and turn to him. A friend who worked in Pakistan told me of a comment made by a Muslim friend of his, that some Christians hated Islam, while other Christians loved Muslims. When we start putting people together as a group, we start stereotyping them and lose sight of them as individuals. And motives can also be a barrier to mission. Are we simply trying to prove that our God is right, or that our religion is better? Or do we act out of love and compassion?

If we have no love or compassion for people, we will not be able to share our faith with them effectively. If we are only concerned with proving that our understanding of God is better than that held by someone else, we will never listen to what motivates our hearer. And if we do not listen, we will never be able to share our faith sensitively and effectively.

Jonah underwent a two-stage reflection and learning process. The lesson on obedience was carried out within the belly of the whale, and the lesson on compassion underneath a castor oil plant. Jonah learnt his lesson about God's compassion when God challenged him about why he cared so much for a castor oil plant that he had not even made, while having no compassion for all the people and animals of Nineveh that God had lovingly created.

Like Jonah, we need to be reminded that we must take the risk of contact with those of other views, and share our faith. But if we have no love, compassion or sensitivity, and we hear God's voice calling, what should we do? Maybe we should take Jonah as our role model and head off in the opposite direction! If we get involved in mission without a compassionate heart, we will be a disaster and end up damaging the work of the Kingdom. Yet even if we set off in the opposite direction, we are at least moving; and if we are moving, there is hope of change. God may take the opportunity to manoeuvre us into a modern-day equivalent of a whale's belly or castor oil plant! There he will be able to work on us and change us, as he did with Jonah, before using us for the furtherance of his Kingdom.

Let us turn now to someone who goes nowhere, someone who wants to follow Jesus but whose offer of service is turned down. The story of the Gerasene demon-possessed man is found in Luke 8:26–39. Can we try to think ourselves into his position?

Have you ever lived among the tombs—a place which feels full of death and hopelessness? I have. Most of us have at some point in our lives. When our lives were full of sin, before we met with Jesus and found eternal life, we lived among the tombs. They are a symbol not of what might have been, but of what was. The people who dwell among the tombs have only a past and no future.

The darkness of the tombs is where ghosts dwell—the ghosts from our sinful past that come back to haunt us, the ghosts from our failures that come back to taunt us. When we dwell among the tombs, we fear the past, because we cannot escape its consequences. The future has nothing in store for us except the prospect of endlessly repeating the mistakes of the past.

While we hate the tombs and desperately wish to escape, perversely we are even more scared of escaping. The tombs are familiar: we have been among them for so long that we do not know how we would cope if we got away. It's far safer to keep close to them and never glimpse the potential of life elsewhere.

Then Jesus comes along. We recognize his authority and, initially, we are scared—not because he will leave us dwelling among the tombs, but because he will try to take us from the tombs. We cry out to resist him. We resent the fact that he might interfere. We are not at all sure that we could cope with the consequences. But Jesus persists, and his authority overcomes all the ghosts and spirits that haunt us. He who breaks down the gates of hell has no trouble breaking our dependency upon sin. He frees us from the past, from dwelling among the tombs.

If we follow him to a new place, we can make a new start. Our lives will be lived out among those who do not know about our past, our failings. People will only know us as we are now. We will not need to explain who we used to be before Jesus met us and freed us. If we stay in our home area, however, we will need to cope with the consequences of our previous sin. It would be so much better to go with Jesus to a new place and make a fresh start as a new person. We beg Jesus to take us with him to a new place. But Jesus wants us to remain in our home area.

It is in our home area, where people knew what we were like before, that we can really witness to the profound changes that Jesus has made to our lives. People who knew us as we were can recognize the power of Jesus in our lives now, and that might help them to think of the difference that Jesus might make to their own lives. It is in our home area, where the tombs are not too far away, that we really find out whether the past is truly behind us or whether in some way it will still determine our future. Through what Jesus has done for us, in delivering us from the tombs, we have been given new life. We need to learn to live that new life within a familiar culture, and it is only when we have done this that we can even begin to consider whether Jesus might want us to follow him to another place.

We begged Jesus to allow us to follow him to a new place, but he refused. Deep down, we knew that he was right to refuse us so soon after our rebirth. Perhaps after we have spent some years living out our new faith within our home area, we might again feel that it is right to follow him to serve him in another place. If so, we can be more confident that we are doing it for the right motives.

Learning about God

Jonah and the demon-possessed man both had to learn more about themselves and about God. Someone else who gives us an example of this is the prophet Hosea, whose experiences are paralleled in a modern example.

The Roman Catholic academic and writer Henri Nouwen, who died in 1996, spent his last few years as a pastor of the L'Arche Daybreak community in Toronto, where he cared for mentally handicapped adults. There was one particular adult, severely handicapped, for whom he spent several hours caring each day. Some people wondered why this famous man could dedicate so much time to such menial work when he could surely use his time more creatively. Nouwen replied that the privilege of looking after this man helped him to understand better the patience that God had for him. Nouwen may have stopped his university teaching but he still applied his academic mind to his everyday experiences.

In any encounter with others, we can respond in three different ways. We can see what we learn about the other person, we can see what we learn about ourselves and we can see what we learn about God. Often we find it less threatening to learn about the other person than to learn about ourselves or about God. Henri Nouwen chose to be in a caring relationship that would be seen by most people as very demanding, something to be avoided or at least minimized. He saw it as an opportunity for learning about God and about himself.

Hosea married Gomer, an ex-prostitute (Hosea 1:2–3). He loved her, but she had no consistency in her love for him and returned to prostitution. Most of us would feel sorry for ourselves in this situation. Hosea realized that his own situation was similar to God's love for Israel and the way that Israel responded to God's love. If Hosea could still love unfaithful Gomer, how much more did God love unfaithful Israel? If Hosea hurt so much from having his love rejected, how much more did God hurt in having his love of Israel rejected?

Anyone going into ministry is going to experience relationship problems. This is particularly true within cross-cultural situations. Apart from the fact that people will behave differently in different cultures, there can be many other potential reasons for relationship difficulties. Working in a different culture can make us vulnerable and insecure, so our own behaviour can be one factor affecting relationships. If we go with an attitude that we are God's gift to the local community, then again we can create relationship difficulties. If we end up working, worshipping and relaxing with the same small group of people, then again stresses can arise.

The real question is not whether we ever have relationship problems, but how we handle them. If we project the whole problem on to the other people, then we will have long-term problems, quite possibly leading to a sticky end. Instead of projecting all the blame on to others, we need to ask ourselves what we could have done differently to have prevented the problem. If we are able to learn about ourselves, then although it might be painful, we may grow and develop personally and end up having a very positive experience. And we also need to follow Hosea's example in allowing the difficult relationship to help us understand how God relates to us. Hosea's experience of a difficult relationship enabled him to see more deeply into the heart of God.

Two words of warning are needed. There is a big difference between using a situation to help us learn about God and putting ourselves in the place of God! We must always avoid the temptation to try to play God in a situation. The second danger, as far as cross-cultural mission is concerned, is assuming that in a different situation we will behave in new and better ways. This is not true. We need to be able to understand ourselves and God within a familiar context before we have any chance of understanding anything within another culture.

Training and temptation

Anyone selected for any kind of ministry is likely to undergo some form of training before beginning that ministry. If we feel that we do not need training, we are considering ourselves as better prepared than Jesus himself! Let us explore his period of training, found in Luke 4:1–13, and see what lessons we can learn from his example.

Jesus' calling is confirmed by a voice from heaven when he is baptized in the Jordan river. Between this confirmation of his calling and his public ministry lies the time in the wilderness. In those days, there were no Bible or theological colleges, but there was plenty of wilderness, and it was a very effective place for training. In those days, they did not think of academic terms, semesters or years, but worked in multiples of forty. The nation of Israel had a forty-year training course and Jesus had forty days. Middle Eastern wildernesses were dry places, and many of us have had wilderness experiences in our lives, times of spiritual dryness. In Jesus' encounter at the well with the Samaritan woman, described in John 4:5–26, he talks of 'living water'. To survive a time of dryness, we need to discover the 'living water' in new ways and put down deeper roots. It is an essential part of training for Christian ministry, as coming through a time of dryness will give us new spiritual resources.

Growth

Leaving our job and home to go into residential training at a Bible college, mission training college or theological college will be a time of being de-professionalized, and this in itself can be a difficult experience as we lose our role and identity. It will be a time of losing some of our role as an individual, or a family, and becoming part of a wider community, and this too can be difficult. It will also be a time of letting go of the restricted vision that we might previously have had of God and his plans for the redemption of his creation, and gaining a deeper understanding. All this can be very threatening. To be effective, training will feel like a wilderness experience at times.

In Matthew 4:1 and Luke 4:1, Jesus is *led* into the wilderness by the Spirit, but in Mark 1:12 he is *driven* into the wilderness by the Spirit. This seems to sum up appropriately the different attitudes that people have towards going into training! Do you see your training for ministry, or mission, as something that you are driven to, or something that you are led to? Perhaps in all of us there are the two elements. We go willingly for the training that we know we need, but we have to be driven by the Spirit for some aspects of preparation. It is probably in the areas where we do not acknowledge our training needs that we most need driving. It might not be pleasant but it is essential that these areas are resolved.

So Jesus went into training for his ministry and he was tempted. This happens to us all when we are in training. Jesus is trying to carry out God's mission and he is tempted to do this in ways that are not appropriate, just as we may be tempted to use means that do not reflect the Kingdom in ministry.

In Matthew 4:3, the temptation is to feed the hungry. Jesus goes into training in the wilderness and grows hungry. He is reminded of the great physical needs of humanity and that one way of drawing humanity back to God is simply to meet people's physical needs. God provided for Israel's physical needs during their wilderness experience, but this is not to be the emphasis of Jesus' mission. His response to this temptation is that 'one does not live by bread alone' (Matthew 4:4a). Mission needs to be holistic, responding to both the physical and the spiritual needs of humanity. We must not give in to the temptation to simplify mission and consider one aspect at the expense of others. We do need bread to live but we also need 'every word that comes from the mouth of God' (Matthew 4:4b).

In Matthew 4:5–7, the devil suggests that Jesus should do something public, spectacular and risky. People will see what happens and will realize that it is only God who could have saved him, proving beyond doubt that God is in Jesus. God worked countless miracles in the past but they never seem to have made any lasting impact upon Israel. This can easily be a temptation that we face—the assumption that if we take risks in God's service then God is duty bound to protect us, which will help people to see the power of God in us. Jesus' reply, in this passage, reminds us that we should not try to put God to the test and depend upon his supernatural powers to convince people of the reality of his power.

In verses 8–11, the devil shows Jesus all the kingdoms of the world and tempts him to take authority over them, by means of worldly power. Jesus, the Son of God, could become a king in the worldly sense of the word. He could introduce a reign more popular than King David and exert an absolute power to bring in the Kingdom of God. Jesus resists this temptation, however, and reminds the devil that we must worship God, and that God's ways are not the ways of the world.

Our temptations in ministry will not be identical to those that Jesus faced, but we can easily be tempted to focus upon one aspect of ministry rather than being holistic; to look more towards the world's values than Kingdom values; to seek supernatural fireworks or to test God. In all three temptations, Jesus is offered the chance of acting in ways in which God has acted in the past history of Israel. All would be ways of showing his divinity and could be legitimate means of bringing people back to God, but this is not how Jesus must carry out his ministry. A life that begins with birth in a stable will lead to the agony and indignity of the cross. A Christian calling is not a calling to privilege but a calling to responsibility and, as it was for Jesus, it will be a calling to vulnerability.

When the devil tempts Jesus, he quotes from a book. It is not another religious text, or the Communist manifesto. That book is the scriptures! As Christians, the danger we face does not come primarily from the writings of other ideologies, but from taking passages of the Bible out of context. Jesus resists temptation because of his knowledge of the scriptures, as he quotes three passages from Deuteronomy to refute the devil. If we too are going to resist temptation during our time of training, we must gain a full knowledge of the Bible so that we see how each passage ties in with the whole message and, with the help of the Holy Spirit, understand its relevance for our ministry today within a given culture.

Growth in relationships

When Jesus was baptized, the Holy Spirit descended upon him (Matthew 3:16). Different Christians will have different understandings about whether there was a growing relationship between the Father and the Son or whether Jesus experienced a leap in understanding of his own identity and ministry at this point. As we enter into a new ministry, we will find that our relationship with God may change. Some will perceive this as a spiritual change, an extra outpouring of the Holy Spirit to enable a new form of ministry. Personally, I find it more helpful to think in terms of the Holy Spirit being at work in stimulating a new relationship between the individual concerned and God. Sometimes it is the awareness of this changed relationship which leads the person to explore a sense of calling. At other times they experience a gradual growth as they test their calling. Some people will be aware of a quantum leap within the relationship. Whilst most ministries are preceded by a training period, some will have a time of retreat and reflection immediately before being admitted to that ministry. This can provide an opportunity to explore further a new relationship with God.

But what of the relationship with the Christian community? For many, their ministry will be within a new Christian community, perhaps in a different country, so this obviously heralds the beginning of new relationships. It can be very different when the ministry is with a community that has known you previously. Again, the calling may come from an awareness of a changing relationship with the community: as the individual takes on greater spiritual responsibilities, the church encourages the individual to consider a formal ministry as a locally ordained minister or as a Reader. Perhaps a new authority to minister will have come about gradually, or the relationship might need a quantum change. Mark 6:1–4 shows the problems that Jesus had in trying to minister amongst his own community. He was seen simply as Mary's son and the brother of James, Joses, Judas and Simon. Faced with this attitude, he was disempowered, and could do hardly any miracles there. This is why it is so important that our calling is confirmed with some kind of rite of passage in the home community, if that is to be the place of the new ministry. We need a commissioning or licensing, or some other rite, whereby our community acknowledges that we have been given authority to minister there in a new way.

In conclusion, let us remind ourselves that growth needs to be taking place at all levels—within our understanding of our calling; in the gaining of relevant talents and experiences; in self-awareness; in biblical understanding; in relationship with God and in relationship to the community where the calling will be lived out.

NOTE
1   *The Good Shepherd*, Mowbray's Christian Studies Series, 1984

CHAPTER 5

Calling and culture

Products of our own culture

We have seen that how we perceive a calling, and how we respond to it, will depend upon the different factors that shape us as individuals, including what is going on around us. An obvious example is found in the story of the call of Isaiah (Isaiah 6:1–9).

In describing his dramatic moment of calling, Isaiah begins with the words, 'In the year that King Uzziah died...'. Isaiah's call is rooted in a particular time in history, the year of the death of King Uzziah—742BC. A calling happens at a particular time in history. The calling comes to someone in a particular nation, and that person is shaped by that nation and by what is going on in the nation at that point in time. Isaiah sets the scene in Isaiah 1:2–4.

Hear, O heavens, and listen, O earth; for the Lord has spoken: I reared children and brought them up, but they have rebelled against me. The ox knows its owner, and the donkey its master's crib; but Israel does not know, my people do not understand. Ah, sinful nation, people laden with iniquity, offspring who do evil, children who deal corruptly, who have forsaken the Lord, who have despised the Holy One of Israel, who are utterly estranged!

And again in Isaiah 1:21–23.

How the faithful city has become a whore! She that was full of justice, righteousness lodged in her—but now murderers! Your silver has become dross, your wine is mixed with water. Your princes are rebels and companions of thieves. Everyone loves a bribe and runs after gifts. They do not defend the orphan, and the widow's cause does not come before them.

The people have forsaken their God, there is widespread bribery and corruption and no longer any justice. Isaiah is a man of his own culture. He describes himself (Isaiah 6:5) as a man of unclean lips, living among a people of unclean lips. We, too, are part of the culture that we live in. We are shaped by that culture and our understanding is shaped by it. Our culture is fallen and we are part of that fallenness.

If God calls you this year, how would you write the story of your call? How would you describe this year? What do you think is the main event by which this year will be remembered? Having identified that, ask yourself what it says about your culture. Does it have implications for you? How would you rewrite Isaiah's 'I am a man of unclean lips, and I live among a people of unclean lips' to apply to your situation? How will people of another culture understand you as a product of your home culture? It is an interesting exercise to try, and one that I have used with groups at vocational conferences.

We are not only shaped by events in our culture at the time of our call; we are also shaped by the period of history that we have lived through. For example, attitudes towards career and professional development will be shaped by the prevailing economic climate. If we chose our career at a time of recession, we are more likely to have opted for security rather than job satisfaction, whereas if the decision was made at a time of high employment, job satisfaction might have been our priority. National events can determine whether we feel pride or embarrassment about our home country. World events can influence whether people are optimistic, pessimistic or cynical about life in general. Those who were students in the late 1960s had an optimism that young people could change things and make a difference. This was countered ten years later by the cynicism of the 'punk generation'. The views of one generation can, to some extent, be a reaction against the views of the previous generation.

The word that Isaiah chooses to describe his culture is 'unclean'. Possibly this is a reference to what is ritually unclean, but the examples that I have quoted from Isaiah 1 show the lies, deception, corruption, greed and injustice that came from people's lips, instead of an acknowledgment of their God. Our own culture shapes our attitudes to what is 'clean' and what is 'unclean'. In this context, it is worth considering the issue of meat offered to idols in Romans 14. In Paul's culture at that time, animals were dedicated to pagan gods while being slaughtered. The issue facing members of the Church was whether or not they could eat such meat. Paul was clear that there is only one God, the Father of our Lord Jesus Christ, and as far as he was concerned, the animal had either been dedicated to that one true God or it had not been dedicated to any god at all. For him person-ally, there was no problem, but he was also aware that many new Christians might still be confused. While they worshipped the Father of our Lord Jesus Christ, they might still believe that other gods existed and had some power. If so, eating meat offered to these deities would be a form of paying homage. For them it would be wrong—a sin. The dilemma for Paul was that if he ate such meat, others might follow his example and eat it too. If they ate it in the knowledge that there was only one God, then fine. But if they did so still believing that other gods existed, they would be sinning and his example would have led them into sin.

In our Western culture, we tend to place the most importance on ourselves and our relationship with God, but Paul says that the focus should be on not only ourselves and 'our' God, but ourselves and the whole people of God. If my action leads someone else to sin, that is wrong and sinful. If we go into another culture, we need to consider carefully what might be the equivalent of meat offered to idols—what might be seen as unclean or wrong by other Christians.

We have attitudes to alcohol, tobacco, clothing, music, dancing and physical contact that we take for granted but which would be considered wrong in some other cultures, while some behaviour that is acceptable within other cultures might shock us. It is essential that we follow Paul's example, working out what might offend and refraining from such behaviour.

Of course our cultural baggage does not stop us from saying, 'Here I am, Lord. Send me.' We should, however, try to understand how our cultural background might influence our sense of calling. Foreign travel, particularly beyond the confines of Europe, has become far more common than previously. In recent years, people have become increasingly accustomed to flying off to another continent for a few days of meetings or conferences. Holidays to exotic locations are within the reach of more people. We need to ask ourselves whether we are really called to another country or whether we are thinking along those lines because it is a comparatively easy thing to do these days. Is our calling, in fact, to those same nationalities who are actually living in British inner cities?

How much has our culture shaped our expectations for job satisfaction? Our standard of living? Our health provision? Our children's education? How much does it affect the expectations that others have of us? Isaiah was profoundly aware that his own culture shaped him. If we are going to hear clearly what God is saying to us, we need to understand how we are shaped by our own culture and how it might affect the way in which we perceive a sense of calling.

What is culture?

Before exploring relevant Bible passages further, it is worth looking more deeply at what we mean by 'culture'. You may find the following diagram helpful.

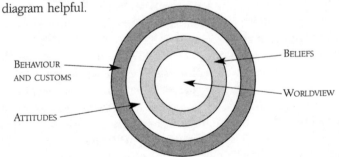

BELIEFS

BEHAVIOUR
AND CUSTOMS

WORLDVIEW

ATTITUDES

When we first go into any culture, the first things we notice are the *behaviour and customs* of that culture—the ways in which things tend to be done. But there is a whole series of values and virtues within every culture. Discovering a culture is like sucking a gobstopper or peeling an onion. As we get beneath the surface, we find the next layer, which is the collection of *attitudes* that shape the behaviour and customs.

Often the attitudes will have influenced the language. I gather that, in Urdu, there is no word for describing a friend of the opposite gender. I remember visiting a married couple in Pakistan, both of whom I had known individually before their marriage, but the wife was now unable to describe me to her language teacher as her friend, only as her husband's friend. In Kiswahili, there is no verb 'to have'. You cannot describe yourself as 'possessing' an object but only as 'being with' an object. You can begin to imagine the impact of these linguistic differences upon the idea of cross-gender friendships in Pakistan and upon attitudes to possessions in parts of East Africa.

Attitudes can also influence institutions. In the last year or so, there has been talk in Britain about 'institutional racism'. This does not mean that individuals are trying to be racist but that a whole structure has been set up based upon attitudes and assumptions that will lead to racist behaviour.

Attitudes do not just happen, however. They are shaped by the next layer of our gobstopper. They are the result of *beliefs*. If a culture has attitudes which are racist or sexist, this reflects the belief that a certain ethnic group, or one of the genders, is inferior. If a society puts an emphasis upon relationships as more important than achievements, this will reflect what people believe in that culture.

Digging deeper, we need to work out what it is that determines the belief system. This is what is known as a *worldview*. A worldview is an understanding of how everything came to be and how the relationships between everything have been arrived at. For Christian and Jewish believers, the first eleven chapters of Genesis explain how creation happened and how the created world was good before it was corrupted by sin. Such a worldview shows that creation has the potential to be good again. In the novel *The Troublesome Offspring of Cardinal Guzman* by Louis de Bernières, a priest describes an alternative worldview.[1] His world is created by Satan. Adam and Eve are angels who have been tricked by Satan and trapped within the mortal bodies that he has created. With this worldview, all creation is seen as flawed or evil and flesh is seen as wicked, so that all we can do is to await death as an opportunity to escape back to heaven. It is easy to imagine how such a worldview might influence beliefs, attitudes and behaviour. Louis de Bernières's characters believe that God is powerless to redeem such a fallen world, so they have a fatalistic and pessimistic attitude and make no attempt to improve fallen behaviour.

The Christian and Jewish worldviews have common starting points, but further developments in these two faiths lead on to other differences. Those who claim to have no faith or philosophy still have a worldview. If you believe that life came about with a random big bang and that there is no God and no overall purpose to creation, then your belief system will reflect this. If you believe that absolute truth is unknowable and that all values are relative, this influences your beliefs, attitudes and behaviour. Our individual worldviews are further shaped by our personal histories, including (as we have already mentioned) the events that were going on at key periods during our lives.

But worldview is rarely static; it is affected by reflection on what is happening in the world. Martyn and Lynn Snow, CMS mission partners in Guinea, West Africa, wrote a prayer letter to their supporting churches describing the way in which people are able to live simultaneously in two totally different cultures. Their reflection was initiated by overhearing a businessman, dressed in a suit worthy of Savile Row, ringing his sorcerer on his mobile phone before agreeing a business deal. They went on to write:

The incident caused us to reflect on the way traditional African culture is clashing head on with Western technology and leaving in its wake much confusion and uncertainty. Sorcerers who work by mobile phone; city dwellers who cook their meals on wood fires while watching French programmes on satellite TV; villagers who come to the clinic to buy sophisticated drugs for illnesses they say are caused by a curse someone has put on them; schoolchildren who have no textbooks but who receive lessons broadcast over the radio. The clash of cultures is everywhere. It is not just mission partners who suffer from culture shock!

Gospel and culture

If we are called to minister within another culture, it helps to understand what might happen when the gospel is taken from one culture to another. A useful example is found in Acts 10, the story of Peter's involvement in the coming to faith of Cornelius and his household. We also have a subplot—what could be described as the conversion of Peter himself. As Peter shares his faith outside his own culture, he has to engage with a number of different issues which transform his outlook. The conversion of Cornelius sounds easy and straightforward but Peter's experience is more painful and complicated.

By the time we have read through the Acts of the Apostles as far as this story, a large number of people have been converted to the gospel message. Virtually all of them have one thing in common: they are Jewish. Some are Greek Jews (who are those living in dispersed Jewish communities within other countries rather than in Judea), but they are still Jewish in terms of their culture and beliefs. The only exception appears to be as a result of Philip's work (Acts 8), which has been mentioned earlier. Although Christianity is expanding, it is in danger of remaining as just another Jewish sect. The story of Peter and Cornelius shows us some of the issues raised when the gospel crosses cultures.

In Acts 10:1–8 we are introduced to Cornelius, a Roman centurion. He believes in the one true God of Judaism, prays to him and gives generously to good causes, but he has not taken the step of embracing Judaism. This would involve circumcision and full adherence to all of the Jewish rituals and rules found within the Law. God responds to his seeking and tells him in a vision to send messengers to fetch Peter from the town of Joppa. In Acts 10:9–16, God prepares Peter for the coming encounter. This will be a far more complex task than the preparation of Cornelius. Peter is a good Christian who knows his scriptures (what we would know as the Old Testament) well. Culturally he is Jewish and his interpretation of scripture, like yours or mine, is determined by his culture. If we concentrate upon specific biblical texts that fit our cultural views, it is easy to lose sight of the 'big picture' and the deeper biblical principles and truths.

From their reading of the message of the Old Testament, the Jews believed that the other nations were quite outside of the mercy of God. Peter knew the Law well enough to be aware of the limitations of social contact that he would be allowed with Gentiles. Gentiles were seen as ritually unclean, and contact with one would make him unclean as well. If he had any concept of Gentiles joining the Christians, his understanding would have been that they needed to become Jews first of all.

This story has three main characters: Cornelius, Peter and the Holy Spirit. The first task for the Holy Spirit is to break down the barriers that will stop Peter from having social contact with Cornelius. This, as we saw when considering Peter in chapter 2, is something that had already started to happen. The Holy Spirit has broadened Peter's understanding of the nature of uncleanness, and this continues to happen through Peter's vision.

In Acts 10:17–23, the Spirit explains the vision and the task to Peter. By the time Cornelius' messengers arrive, we see that the barriers are already starting to be broken down as Peter invites them in and offers them hospitality for the night. This is something that, culturally, he would not have been allowed to do for non-Jews. Then Peter travels to Caesarea (Acts 10:24–43) with the messengers and some of the other believers and, after the lessons of the previous day, he enters Cornelius' house. Peter and Cornelius then both share the stories of what God has just done in their lives and how he has spoken to them. Peter goes on to explain the gospel message to Cornelius and his household, beginning with his own new revelation that God accepts people from every nation.

As Peter reaches the end of his sermon, he faces a new dilemma. These people are obviously accepting the good news of Jesus. What does he do next? Does he now have to explain Judaism to them and insist upon their acceptance of that, and circumcision, before they can be baptized as Christians? Again it is time for the Holy Spirit to make an appearance. In Acts 10:44–48, Cornelius and his household are baptized in the Spirit. This, in the past, has only happened after baptism in water and only to those who were Jewish. Peter realizes that if they can be baptized in the Spirit, then they must be acceptable to God without a prior conversion to Judaism. His dilemma has been answered and he goes ahead with baptizing them in water, spending another few days with them and giving them further Christian instruction.

Peter's own understanding of God's purpose in salvation was too small. It needed to grow, and growing can be a painful and difficult process. It can mean letting go of familiar landmarks and assumptions and reaching out in faith, trusting that we are being held and guided by the Holy Spirit, to find a bigger vision of God. Sharing Christ in a cross-cultural situation is not the sharing of a gift-wrapped package. It means telling our story of how God has worked in our life and, like Peter, listening to the other person's story. The other person's story may well challenge my faith in ways that I had not expected.

If I try to share my faith with a Muslim or Hindu, I will encounter stumbling blocks, whether or not they accept Christ. I cannot ignore those stumbling blocks, but I must allow God to be big enough to overcome them for me. If I speak to someone who cannot accept Christianity because they cannot see how God has allowed a particular event to happen, then I cannot ignore that question. Even if I cannot convince them of the answer, I must find an answer that satisfies me or I am *en route* to losing my own faith. Sharing our faith can be a risky and painful process, but if we are doing so at the prompting of the Holy Spirit we will be guided through the process and emerge on the other side, like Peter, with a new and deeper vision of God.

Cross-cultural insights

When we enter another culture, we often find ourselves able to look at an aspect of that culture and see it in a different way from those around us. What we have at this stage is a 'cultural insight'. We are looking around us with the understanding that we have from our own background, which gives us a different perspective compared to those who have always lived within that culture. We must remember, however, that although we may have this ability we must exercise it with discretion. Sometimes, we might not be seeing the reality of a situation but might actually be seeing things that are not really there!

When we look at an aspect of our own familiar context, it can be like looking at it with just one eye. We can see what is there but we lose any sense of perspective. Looking at something within another culture will, in fact, be the same. We will notice things that others perhaps ignore, but we still lack perspective because we do not understand the assumptions behind local traditions and may misunderstand what we are seeing. I may judge another person's bad time-keeping as being inefficiency, rather than realizing that it reflects a culture in which relationships are valued so highly that people spend all the time they need with someone else before moving on to the next appointment.

We need to be able to look at something with two eyes at once! This gives us a three-dimensional view, so that we can see it fully and appreciate it in its true perspective. It is not as simple as having two different people looking at the same thing from two different cultural perspectives. People with different outlooks need to work together in partnership. They need to look at things together, and share their insights with each other. Working in partnership in this way changes our cultural perspectives into a God-given gift.

This is one of the main reasons why God calls people to cross cultural boundaries and get involved in mission. It is not just about what we can do for each other, it is about the insights that we can share with each other. It is so easy to go around looking at things from our own point of view and ending up with only half the picture. Of course, we do it all the time within our own culture and forget that we need Christians from elsewhere to give us their insights, so that we can get a true picture of what is happening in our own society.

Jeremiah's ministry did not start with action. It started with the prophet looking around him and describing what he saw (Jeremiah 1:11–13). This is a good way for anyone to start his or her ministry. It can be very tempting just to get on with things but first of all we need to get the full picture and to find out what God is saying.

When we have learnt how to see things through the eyes of others and work together in partnership, we can return home with the ability to see things from different perspectives. Our culture will never look the same again. This is a very powerful gift to bring back with us, but it might take a little time to 'focus' properly and put things in perspective. As with any spiritual gift, our insights are best tested with Christian leadership before being acted upon!

Having our assumptions challenged

Ministering within another culture can challenge some of our most basic attitudes. A particular example is our attitude to success.

'Success' is very much a word of our times and our Western culture. People want to talk about their success, not about their failure. We hope to be successful in finding employment. We try to be successful in our work, successful in our family lives, successful in our other relationships. Perhaps we look for a successful church to join. We want to be successful in what we do for God—successful in mission. So let's look for a New Testament example of successful mission.

If I look in my Bible concordance to find the word 'success', I learn an interesting lesson. 'Succeed', 'success' and 'successful' are not New Testament words. These words appear a few times in the Old Testament but never in the New. On the page of my concordance where I expect to find references to 'success', I find instead references to 'suffer'. 'Suffer' is a New Testament word but 'success' is not.

In Matthew 14:29–33 we have a story of Jesus calling Peter to do something. By the end of those four short verses, Jesus is being worshipped as the Son of God. Surely Peter must have done something very successfully for this to happen? In fact, Matthew tells us, he tried to walk on water, started to sink and was saved by Jesus. It was Peter's lack of success in human terms which led to success in godly terms. Jesus can transform failure in worldly terms to success in terms of the Kingdom.

Peter was trying to understand this experience of apparent failure before the events of the crucifixion and resurrection had taken place. Since we, with the benefit of hindsight, know what Jesus achieved through his death, we should never forget that God is most powerful in vulnerability. God challenges our worldly values and turns them upside down. His success will often be in our failure.

Paul writes in 1 Corinthians 1:22–23, 'For Jews demand signs and Greeks desire wisdom, but we proclaim Christ crucified, a stumbling block to Jews and foolishness to Gentiles.' We need to preach Christ crucified before we can preach Christ risen. Often the people we encounter will need to identify with our human weaknesses and failures before they can recognize and worship the God who works through our human frailty and who can transform our failures into success in terms of his Kingdom.

Of course, Peter did manage to walk on water for a few steps, carried through by his faith and enthusiasm in responding to the call from Jesus. It was only after those first few steps that he became conscious of the wind and became afraid and started to sink. Those who respond to a calling must be prepared to face that sinking feeling. They, too, must be ready to be pulled down or broken, or humiliated, or to find that their faith is not strong enough for a particular situation. But, like Peter, they too will know that Jesus is there to save them. If Peter had succeeded in walking on the water in his own strength, who would have received the praise—Peter or Jesus?

I am reminded of an irreverent but relevant story. A vicar and his curate are having a day fishing from a boat on a lake with the visiting bishop. At different times both the vicar and the curate have to return to land for something and the bishop is amazed to see them walking back to shore across the water. When it comes to the bishop's turn to go back to the lakeside, he has to assure them that he has as much faith as they do, so he steps on to the water and immediately sinks. The curate turns to his vicar and says, 'Did the bishop not know about the submerged stepping stones?'

In this story, the 'walking on the water' is not a miracle caused by faith, but an illusion caused by an extra bit of knowledge. Sometimes when we go to serve God in another culture, by virtue of our education, background or culture we take that extra bit of knowledge with us. We might be especially welcomed because of this extra bit of knowledge and the contribution that it can help us to make. We need to be careful that our special skill does not look in some way like a miracle and cause people to start to worship our knowledge, technology or culture, rather than the God who gave us the knowledge in the first place.

Of course, mission does include sharing God-given knowledge. But ultimately it will mean sharing the knowledge and experience of God's saving power through Jesus Christ. We make it very difficult for God's power to shine through if we are trying to demonstrate our own strengths. This is why the New Testament does not use the word 'success'. Frailty and failure in human terms can be transformed to success by God.

The whole set-up of Jesus' ministry challenges our cultural assumptions. Imagine that you are about to start an international company. You have three years to get this company up and running. After three years you intend to hand the business over to colleagues to continue on your behalf. You may choose twelve colleagues to help you run the company. So what type of people would you choose? Looking at this question helps us to understand better not only how Jesus organized his ministry but also the type of people he was calling to be involved.

I know what kind of people I would choose. I would try to attract some of the big names from show-business, sport, commerce and government. I would choose people from the media and possibly one person who was good at accountancy to look after the money. It would be good to have some people with management skills and some people with teaching skills, perhaps someone from the academic world.

However I look at it, I cannot see myself appointing any fishermen to my team. Not even one. So why did Jesus choose so many fisher-men to be his disciples? I can understand the choice of Matthew— a tax collector would be quite good as accountant and probably had useful contacts among the Romans. Judas Iscariot might have had some good connections to the revolutionaries on the other side of the political spectrum. But what skills or gifts did fishermen have that made them so useful for Jesus? After all, Jesus compared mission with fishing and said that he would make these disciples 'fishers of people'.

The first quality that fishermen have is faith. The whole point of fishing is that you cannot see what is beneath the water. Fishing means going ahead in the belief that there is something there and that you will see it in the fullness of time. When you look at water, both reflection and refraction affect what you see. You try to see under the water, but instead you are dazzled by reflected images of your surroundings instead. To be a fisherman, you must not be blinded by such distractions but must hold on to your faith that the fish are there, waiting to be caught.

Once you get past the distracting reflections, you still have to deal with the refraction. Even if you can see the fish, or anything else under the water, they will not be as they seem. The water itself distorts the light so that size and position are subtly altered. Once again, as a good fisherman you must not be confused by such distortions but must focus on what really lies there under the surface.

Fishermen are aware that once you have caught a fish, you need to do something with it. Those fishermen called by Jesus would have realized the importance of making disciples of those they brought to faith. We, too, must be aware that if we bring people to faith we must do this as part of a church that can develop them as Christians. Any analogy breaks down if taken too far, and this is true of the analogy of fishing. However, any fisherman will know that if you do nothing after you catch your fish, you have what can be referred to as 'a fish out of water'. And if you catch a fish and put it back, that fish will be much harder to catch a second time.

Trying to be incarnate

When we go to minister within another culture, we are forced to ask ourselves how deeply we can ever identify with, and be accepted by, the other culture. I remember the circumstances that led me specifically to reflect upon this.

I was to preach on Advent Sunday, which would be immediately after my return from an overseas visit, so it seemed appropriate to look at the three readings in the Anglican lectionary well in advance and mull them over while I went for my pre-visit inoculations. The Old Testament lesson was Isaiah 52:7–10, which includes these words:

> *The Lord has bared his holy arm*
> *before the eyes of all the nations;*
> *and all the ends of the earth shall see*
> *the salvation of our God.*

Somehow, as I dutifully rolled up my sleeve, I found myself reflecting upon what was really meant by God baring his holy arm. It was obviously God having his inoculations! The passage foretells God's incarnation in the person of Jesus Christ, and so God was preparing himself for his visit to Israel by having the right inoculations. I could almost imagine the comments of the doctor at the surgery. 'Going to Israel? You'd better have tetanus and typhoid. Bethlehem—occupied territory. Right, you need to have something for hepatitis as well. Do keep away from animals and dirty stables, make no contact with those who have contagious diseases, and avoid rusty nails.'

It was at that point that the imagery broke down. The incarnate God did not keep away from animals and dirty stables. He sought out those with contagious diseases and had contact with them. In particular, he did not avoid those rusty nails. The God that I believe in, who was incarnate as Jesus Christ, is not the sort of God who takes a lot of precautions. He's more the sort of God who rolls up his sleeves and gets involved.

Rolls up his sleeves? 'Bared his holy arm'! The phrase is also used in Psalm 98 to describe a time when God has intervened to win a victory for Israel. Isaiah believes in a God who does get involved. He is foretelling the incarnation, the birth of Jesus. God continues to roll up his sleeves and get involved with his creation. One way in which he does it is to continue calling people to be involved in his mission.

What does Jesus' incarnational involvement in the world say to my cautious approach? Now, don't get me wrong. I am not saying that you do not need to have inoculations before going to work abroad. Only if your calling is to martyrdom, rather than to service, are inoculations unnecessary!

The Father sends the Son to be God incarnate, to be involved in the world and to identify with people. Jesus is both God and man and enters into our humanity with all of its sorrows, joys and pains. If we are called to serve God in a cross-cultural situation, we are equally called to be involved in the life of the people. We are called to be God's love incarnate. We need to remember, however, that Jesus was both God and man and that we are only human. We do need to try to be incarnational in our involvement in mission but to remember that we are not God and that we will not be able to be fully incarnational. On the one hand we should follow Jesus' model of incarnation; on the other hand we will inevitably be limited by how much we can identify with the people whom we go to serve. We need God's discernment to wrestle with the issues involved.

Should I be paid more than my national counterpart? Do I have to have a higher standard of living? Would I relate to my national colleagues more closely if I shared their lifestyle more closely? Should my children go to the same school as local children? Should my family make do with the same medical provision as the national Christian community? Do I stay if there is a civil war? Am I in some way putting God to the test?

I am not going to provide the answers for you. Different mission agencies might have different answers to some of these questions, and some you will need to work out for yourself, listening carefully and prayerfully to the views of others. We are called to be incarnational, but just how incarnational? These are difficult and often painful questions to wrestle with—potentially much more painful than inoculations.

Another important issue when going into another culture is to make an honest assessment of the support systems that you require and whether you will be able to find such support.

Calling and culture

As we have already seen, the story of Abram's call into the unknown is often held up as an example that we should be prepared to follow. If we look carefully at the text in Genesis 12:5, however, we see that 'Abram took his wife Sarai and his brother's son Lot, and all the possessions that they had gathered, and the persons whom they had acquired in Haran; and they set forth to go to the land of Canaan'.

Perhaps the biblical lesson is that if you do go somewhere completely unknown, make sure that you take all your support systems with you! This is hardly practical in modern-day mission situations, so careful thinking beforehand is needed. Are you going to be able to support yourself financially in your new situation? Will you, as an individual person or a family unit, have the personal support that you need to survive and flourish? The spiritual support that you need to survive and grow as a Christian? Appropriate health facilities for you and your family? Education facilities for your children?

Going to be involved in cross-cultural mission means, to some extent, going into the unknown. We will never get all of the facts. We may know the facts as they apply at one particular point in time to one particular person, but they will change. There will always be an element of faith, but the God who gives us our faith also gives us our ability to reason and to seek information and process it. Determining whether we feel called to a situation will be a combination of our response to both faith and facts.

In helping people to explore whether or not they have a vocation to cross-cultural mission, I try to determine how someone will cope with a particular situation. Sometimes people respond by saying, 'If God wants me to go to that situation, then God will provide me with the resources to cope.' Basically I agree with them, but I choose to phrase it differently. I reply, 'If God has provided you with the resources to cope with a particular situation, then he might be calling you to that location.' Taking that as my starting point, I try to help the person to explore how they might cope in a given situation. In doing this, we need an understanding of how people have coped with situations in the past and how they have learnt and grown as a result.

You will go into any exploration of a vocation with questions that you will want answered. You will want to know facts, so that you can determine whether or not a particular location is right for you. The agency considering you will need to explore all sorts of things about you. They will want facts to understand how you have functioned in the past and how you have grown and changed, so that they can try to predict how you might function in the future. When both you and the agency have considered all the facts, both can decide in faith whether it appears that God is calling you to go ahead. The process may be very different from the one that Abraham went through but it will be a calling, in faith, to follow in the tradition of Abraham and to be part of the same mission that he was called to.

NOTE
1   Page 30 (published by Vintage Fiction, 1998)

CHAPTER 6

The tensions of the tasks

As we have already seen, mission involves a tension between being in close contact with a culture and retaining the distinctive Christian message and worldview. As we look more closely at specific types of Christian ministry, we begin to notice inherent tensions within them. These tensions, in turn, bring questions to our faith and its out-working. If you are called to such a ministry, you must be confident that you can cope with such tensions. Some people will be stimulated by those kinds of challenges and this stimulus might be part of their sense of leading. For others, such issues will need careful exploration before they can decide whether or not their own calling should embrace those challenges. While the examples I give reflect my own work with CMS, the tensions themselves can be encountered in ministry within any country.

Christianity and other faiths

Whether your ministry is in your own country or abroad, you will probably come into contact with people of other faiths. In present-day cultures, there is a tension between the assumption that we can never know 'objective truth' and the claim of Jesus Christ, in John 14:6, that 'I am the way, and the truth, and the life. No one comes to the Father except through me.' In a post-colonial period, as we reflect upon some of the racist attitudes that resulted from a sense of cultural superiority, it is hard to reconcile Jesus' claim with the prevailing view that all faiths are equally valid, a view akin to the Hindu understanding that all paths lead to God. While in many ways this view is an attractive proposition, sounding generous, accepting and open-minded, if I take it as my starting point, then, personally, I cannot make sense of the cross. If all paths are equally valid, the cross was unnecessary, salvation could have been achieved by some other means and, to me, the crucifixion becomes a cruel joke.

There will be a whole range of views about where other faiths come from. There will be different views about how much good there is within them, whether or not God can be found in any way within them, how much we can learn about our own faith from them, and how God responds to those who believe in them. It would need a whole book to do justice to such issues. I personally believe that something happened upon the cross that had not happened before and has not happened since, which made salvation possible for all people. It made the healing of broken relationships possible for all people and all creation. I also believe that whether other faiths have part of the whole truth or none of it, the good news of Jesus needs to be sensitively shared. In sharing it, I need to take seriously the ways in which other people, of other faiths, relate their understanding of God to their life experiences. While I cannot accept that there is no objective truth, I can accept that I might not personally have the full truth and that I need to share my views with humility and with openness to the fact that I can learn about God from other people's experiences.

There are different biblical examples of engaging with another faith. Approaches will vary depending upon the context and upon whether there are starting points for dialogue within an existing worldview. Let's look at the example of Paul in Athens, told in Acts 17:16–34. The Athenians were into new ideas and arguing and discussion for the sake of it. We get the impression that philosophy and debate were an intellectual exercise and, whatever the conclusions, it was all in the head and not in the heart. Sometimes we can want others to accept our point of view because we like winning an argument. It boosts our sense of self-worth if we can prove that what we believe is right and what the other person believes is wrong. If we feel like this, we are guilty of wanting the other person to accept our view for the sake of our credibility rather than the credibility of the God whom we worship. These are not good reasons for being involved in dialogue.

Paul, as we are told in verse 16, was motivated by his great distress at seeing the idols, and engaged in dialogue out of compassion caused by this distress. We need to be clear what our motives are before we engage in dialogue and to be sure that they are selfless.

Paul starts off (v. 17) by talking to those who do believe in the God of the Old Testament, to the Jews and the God-fearing Greeks. It is through these discussions that he engages with the Epicurean and Stoic philosophers. Through this encounter, he is invited (v. 19) to go and speak at the meeting of the Areopagus (the Greek for Mars Hill— where a court of no more than 30 people met who, as well as considering cases of homicide, had an oversight of public morals and religious issues). Paul will get an audience there because he has been invited to speak. If we are to be heard, we will need to earn the right to speak, and this will often take time. We do not know why Paul earned the right to speak on this occasion. It might have been because of his eloquence in speaking and arguing a point, but it may well have been because he showed interest in what the philosophers were saying. As we shall shortly see, Paul had certainly understood and engaged with their thinking.

It is no good speaking too soon. If we have not earnt the right to speak, it is likely that nobody will listen to us. Equally, it is pointless to put off speaking indefinitely, just in case the time is not yet right. In finding the right moment, as in so many other things, we need to be sensitive to the leading of the Spirit.

So how does Paul begin his talk? Does he blast the Athenians for their idolatry and sinful nature? No. He starts by praising them for their religious zeal (v. 22). The huge number of idols says something about their enthusiasm for religion, and Paul begins by affirming this. It is a successful method, whatever your message. If you wish to make a point to someone but begin by being critical, they are likely to become defensive. If you start off by praising them, they are likely to listen!

Vincent Donovan, a Roman Catholic missionary who worked with the Masai in Tanzania, paraphrases the words of Paul in his excellent book on cross-cultural mission, *Christianity Rediscovered*:[1] 'Everyone knows how devout you Masai are, the faith you have, your beautiful worship of God. You have known God and he has loved you. But…'. Praising rather than condemning people must not just be a glib exercise, however. It must be built upon an understanding of what we are praising, otherwise it will sound insincere.

Paul explains that he has come across a shrine to an unknown god (v. 23). Six hundred years previously, there had been a severe plague, and to try to halt it, the poet Epimenides had released a flock of black-and-white sheep from the Areopagus into the streets. Wherever one stopped and lay down, it was sacrificed to the god of the nearest shrine. Where there was no shrine, the sheep was sacrificed to 'an unknown god'. Paul proclaims that this unknown god, who has been worshipped for the previous six hundred years, is knowable.

There is a danger in thinking that we have to take God with us into new situations. God has created this world and is already there in his creation. Our task is not to take God with us but to discover where he is already and proclaim him as the God who is the Father of Jesus Christ. Paul explains that this 'unknown god' is knowable, and that he is the God of creation who is not housed within temples and idols.

Vincent Donovan again adopts Paul's methodology and uses the imagery of a national god of the Masai really being the High God of all creation. And in his book *Peace Child*,[2] Don Richardson describes his work with the Sawi people of Netherlands New Guinea. This culture appeared to be one with no obvious starting point to share Jesus until the workers discovered that reconciliation between warring factions could come about only by each party giving a child to the other party. From this, the missionaries were able to show that God gave Jesus, the ultimate Peace Child, to reconcile himself with his creation. Dialogue is not a matter of bringing in an opposing God, bigger and better than the existing one. It is showing that the existing God is bigger and better than has previously been assumed, and can be experienced more fully through Jesus Christ.

In Athens, Paul wishes to make the point that we are all God's offspring. Rather than using his own scriptures to do this, Paul quotes from the poem 'Phainomena' by Aratus. His hearers do not know or accept Paul's scriptures and will not be impressed or influenced by them. If we are to engage with people of another faith, we should try to use pointers from their own holy books to point to our Christian understanding of God. There is, however, a danger in 'using' their scriptures. We cannot just take quotes out of context to make our point, because this is patronizing, insulting and, ultimately, damaging to our cause. It is important to know the context of the quotation and how it is traditionally understood. To do this, we must try to see and understand things the way the other person does. It is essential to take their beliefs and experiences seriously and empathize with their understanding.

The late Jeremy Hinds was a CMS mission partner engaging with Islam in West Africa and then in Lancashire. He was so well known and accepted by different families and communities in West Africa that he was often asked to pray at weddings and funerals and with sick people. Although he spoke Arabic, he would pray in the local language of Hausa, and this surprised his hearers, as many Muslims believe that Allah can hear prayers only in Arabic.

Jeremy's empathy with Islam highlighted the risks involved in such encounters. I have heard people ask him what was the hardest thing about his work. He would reply, somewhat tongue in cheek, that the hardest thing was not becoming a Muslim! That showed how deeply he empathized. Sharing with those of another faith, if we take their experiences seriously, can be very challenging to our own faith and raise some questions for which we will not necessarily find easy answers. If this is to be our calling, we need to be prepared for it.

The more we look into what Paul was doing in Athens, and Jeremy in West Africa, the more we realize that they were well prepared for their encounters. Of course we should wait upon the prompting of the Holy Spirit, but we should also work as Paul did, using his knowledge of the shrine to the 'unknown god'. He understood the local culture and history and was able to find the right starting point. He also knew the Athenians' literature well enough to find an appropriate quotation to use. Paul was in dialogue with both the Epicureans and Stoics, who each had a totally different understanding of the meaning of life. In looking at Paul's speech (vv. 22–31), it is obvious that he knew their beliefs thoroughly, and also where they would particularly disagree with each other. And his earlier discussions, before his invitation to speak to them, had been an important part of his preparation.

Paul's speech did not produce amazing results. When he finished, some sneered, some wanted to hear more and some became followers. If some do want to hear more, like Paul we have opportunities for more prayerful research and another chance to share our beliefs.

In Athens, Paul had to find the right starting point for his dialogue within the other faith. And we need to do the same in our encounters. The Koran does have a bit to say about Jesus, although we Christians will disagree with much of it. It does mean, however, that Muslims have their own understanding of Jesus. One aspect of this understanding is of Jesus as healer.[3] Mohammed made no such claims about himself. There are many stories of Muslims coming to Christian hospitals because they recognized Jesus as a healer and looked to the healing ministry of the hospital. There are also stories of those who have been healed and have been sure, perhaps through a vision, that it was Jesus who healed them.

Usually the approach to other faiths will be through some form of service. 'The Well', in Glasgow, is a Christian-run information and advice centre for Asian people living locally. Sardar and Violet Ghauri have come from Peshawar in Pakistan to serve there, an arrangement facilitated jointly by the Church of Scotland and CMS. Sardar says, 'The opportunities to get to know many people of Asian background and share with them the love of Jesus Christ in the context of compassionate support—and on occasions directly share with them our Christian faith—are a privilege.'

Felipé Yanez is from Chile. He is being supported jointly by another Anglican agency, the South American Mission Society (SAMS), and CMS. He is involved with two youth clubs in Birmingham. One has thirty members from the Pakistani and Yemeni communities, the other is for children who have links with the local parish church. Perhaps their parents or grandparents attend. Felipé sees them as being the church of tomorrow who need to be nurtured and encouraged. He is also involved in 'Puppet Mundo' (Puppet World), an evangelistic puppet show that shares the gospel in an entertaining way.

Service and evangelism

Another tension that occurs within different types of Christian ministries is the polarization between service and evangelism. We see in Acts 6 that the early Church tried to keep them separate, but Acts 7 and 8 tell how the Holy Spirit had other plans.

With the appointment of the seven deacons, a strategic decision was taken to separate the tasks of evangelism and service—a decision which, in the light of the evangelistic opportunities that two of the deacons then discovered, seemed rather dubious. We know little of what happened to five of the seven deacons, but Stephen and Philip fill the rest of these three chapters with their stories. They are not the stories of people serving at table!

Stephen has been called to be a servant, not an evangelist, but the events that follow show that the two roles cannot be separated. He was appointed to be a servant so that the apostles would have more time to concentrate upon 'prayer and serving the word' (their preaching and teaching ministry mentioned in Acts 6:4). He is described as being full of grace and power, and performs signs and wonders among the people. We may assume that he does 'wait at table', the task described in Acts 6:2 for which he has been chosen. But the impact that he is making stirs up opposition: he has to justify his faith and, in doing so, shows his great wisdom. As a result of this, some people spread lies about him and he is dragged off to court. He is taken before the Jewish council of the elders (Acts 6:12) where, in answer to the accusations made against him, he goes right through Israel's history and shows how its leaders always, without fail, ignored what God was saying to them and did the exact opposite. He points out that every time God sent someone to do his will and proclaim his word, that servant of God was persecuted or killed. He points out that it is the council of elders who are ignoring the law, not him.

Stephen is taken away and stoned to death, and goes down in history as the first Christian martyr. Although he was chosen for service, he is remembered for evangelism—the two tasks are not mutually exclusive. There was powerful Christian witness not only in his words but also in the manner of his death. While giving his speech at the Council, 'his face was like the face of an angel' (Acts 6:15). At his death, he asks Jesus to receive his spirit, and he also asks the Lord to forgive those who are killing him (Acts 7:60).

We do not know the extent of the impact of Stephen's words and death, although we know that one of those present at his execution was Saul. Renewed persecution certainly followed on from Stephen's death, probably sorting out those who were followers because Christianity was an interesting intellectual exercise and those who had a real and meaningful faith. The time of persecution led to dispersion of the Christian community. No longer was Philip part of the ordered life of the Christian group in Jerusalem where his calling was to wait upon table. Instead he found himself in a city in Samaria (Acts 8:5) and started preaching the word there. It is worth pausing to consider the significance of this.

Samaria corresponded to much of the old northern kingdom of Israel. When the northern kingdom was taken into exile by Assyria in the eighth century BC, it lost its cultural and religious identity. Those northerners who had been exiled to Assyria and those who were left in Israel intermarried with Gentiles and developed a faith that mixed elements of Judaism with other faiths. In contrast, those from the old southern kingdom of Judah were taken into exile by Babylon in the following century and managed to keep their cultural and religious identities pure. Much of the understanding of who the Jewish people were developed through this exile experience. After Judah returned from exile, a deep hatred grew between the Jews and the Samaritans.

As far as the Samaritans were concerned, they were still descendants of Abraham and worshipped the same God. As far as the Jews were concerned, the Samaritans were a hybrid people with hybrid religious practices, worshipping a hybrid god. If the Jews were to acknowledge anything good about the Samaritans, then they would be watering down their own identity and beliefs. Far better a Gentile who knew he was Gentile than a Samaritan who thought that he was related to you and pretended that he worshipped the same God!

Until the persecution after Stephen's death, all of those who had become Christians were practising Jews. Some were Hellenistic (Greek-speaking) Jews from elsewhere in the Roman Empire, but they were ethnically Jewish and practised the Jewish faith. Some might have been proselytes, like Nicolaus (Acts 6:5)—ethnically not Jewish, but people who had deliberately converted to Judaism.

It is Philip, chosen to be a servant rather than an evangelist, who starts to convert the Samaritans. But he does not stop there! At the direction of an angel of the Lord, Philip goes off to the road between Jerusalem and Gaza and, as we have already considered, encounters a Gentile—the Ethiopian official returning home from worship at Jerusalem (Acts 8:26–39). The Church makes a division between evangelism and service. The Holy Spirit seems to recognize no such division. Of these two servants, Stephen and Philip, one becomes the first martyr because of his evangelism. The other is responsible for taking the gospel not just to the Samaritans, but also to an Ethiopian official, who probably shares the gospel on his return home, playing a part in bringing into being the ancient Coptic church of Egypt and the Ethiopian church which developed from it.

Sadly, many people still feel that you can separate out service and evangelism. Thankfully, the Holy Spirit is still showing that you cannot. Sometimes, like Stephen, it will be your actions as a Christian that will make people ask questions. Sometimes, like Philip, people will question you because they know that you are a Christian, and you will find that the Holy Spirit has changed your role for you. If those who go to serve find that they are also sharing the word, it is worth commenting that those who go to share the word should also expect to serve. Often it will be the servant heart that gives credibility to the message.

Nowadays, most of those who go as mission partners will be going with the qualifications and experience needed for serving the people that they go to, as well as seeking sensitive ways to share their faith. This is particularly true of long-term service, as few governments would offer a work permit to someone whose only task was to be an evangelist. Here are some examples from CMS's responses to requests from partner churches.

English is usually the second language that many people want to learn. I read recently that the number of Chinese people enrolled on English language courses is greater than the combined populations of Canada and the United States of America. CMS has sent Gail Philip as a mission partner to teach at a diocesan language centre in Bangkok, Thailand. Gail has one young adult class (13–16 year olds) and three adult classes. The language centre gives students access to the church and some are keen to hear more about being a Christian. Any profit the centre makes is channelled back into a community service project that runs a variety of ministries to support the poor and the marginalized.

A mission partner couple is based in Sudan. The wife, as well as being a homemaker, teaches at an English language school. The husband is involved in Christian-based development work. As well as encouraging the diocesan development officers from each diocese, he has been involved in a training programme in small-scale business practices. Although this has only small beginnings, people are appreciating the training and are seeing it as a way to help themselves rather than being dependent on outside donors.

Mike and Tracey Walmsley, a water engineer and dentist respectively, are with CMS in rural Nepal. Mike is teaching water engineering to second-year students. The actual teaching plus the lesson preparation take up half of his time. The rest of the time, he works with three local staff in the outlying villages on community development projects such as pit latrine construction and drinking water systems. Tracey is involved in dental camps in outlying villages and providing training at the local hospital.

Peter and Mandy Greenwood have worked for the last five years with CMS in Islamabad, the capital of Pakistan, Peter as vicar of St Thomas' church. Mandy has had opportunity to be involved in St Thomas' Community Care for the Disabled project. This works in four of Islamabad's squatter settlements that are largely inhabited by Christian families. These people live on low incomes in small, basic houses with the insecurity of their squatter status. They have little chance of formal education or access to reliable health information or health care. When a disabled person is added to the family, despair can easily set in. Mandy saw families' attitudes to the disabled changing, and this in turn started to affect the attitudes of others in the settlements. The project has trained eight of the women living in the four settlements, who previously had only basic school education. They operate as care workers to support families affected by disability. The project has given a sense of hope to many families, who were otherwise facing despair.

Centripetal or centrifugal mission

There is a tension at the heart of much of Christian service which reflects different styles of mission. In the Old Testament, Israel is called to be a light to the nations, and in Isaiah 56:6–7 we are presented with the imagery of the nations coming to the holy mountain and also of God's house being a house of prayer for all nations. Old Testament mission can be viewed as centripetal, flowing *into the centre*. In the New Testament, the Church is called to go out to the nations. Mission is centrifugal, flowing *out from the centre* in all directions. With centripetal mission, people are brought to a God who is found at the centre. With centrifugal mission, God is taken to a people who dwell at the perimeter, who dwell at the margins.

I have visited Vellore Christian Medical College and Hospital in India. It is one of the biggest teaching hospitals in Asia and patients come to it not just from all over India but also from the subcontinent and the surrounding countries. Within a few miles of Vellore, you could encounter some of the worst health problems in India. The hospital directors realized that they could not simply expect people to come in to be cured; they needed to go out into the villages, find the root causes of disease and tackle them. The Rural Unit for Health and Social Affairs was developed under the leadership of Dr Daleep Mukarji, now Director of Christian Aid in Britain. This unit established literacy programmes and teaching on nutrition, agricultural development schemes and small businesses, which helped to tackle the poverty that was the root cause of the health problems. It also founded clinics to meet specific health needs.

Traditionally, hospitals and other institutions will reflect the Old Testament centripetal style of mission, where people are expected to come in to the centre to have their needs met. The initiative taken at Vellore represents a shift to centrifugal mission, with resources from the centre being taken out to meet people where they are within the community. Over the years, CMS has increasingly responded to primary healthcare initiatives, sending medics to preventative work within the community rather than curative work in hospitals.

This centrifugal approach is also effective in rural development work such as the work of Mike Walmsley. It is also found within theological education. Adrian and Jill Chatfield have been sent jointly by another Anglican agency, Crosslinks, and CMS to work in theological education by extension (TEE) in southern Africa. This method, increasingly used in the West as well, involves people in study locally, while remaining within an existing job, rather than in a college environment. Training is thus related to the local context rather than remaining as abstract learning. Adrian is involved in writing new courses and rewriting some existing courses, while Jill visits the regional co-ordinators.

The national church in a given country will often prefer an institutional (centripetal) approach, which traditionally builds standards of excellence, while the Western mission partner will prefer the centrifugal, locally based approach. The reality is that there continues to be a need for both.

While CMS often sends qualified people to help with theological training for new, rapidly growing churches in Africa, for example, a recent development has been to send mission partners to work with one of the older churches, the Russian Orthodox. This Church was allowed to continue its training of clergy during the Communist era, but was banned from encouraging faith to engage with society and from teaching children. Penny and Robin Minney have been training Religious Education teachers and Sunday school teachers in Moscow.

Both have written textbooks to follow up their work. Robin's book is based upon his lectures on Religious Education and Penny is editing a book of talks from a conference on Religion and Literature.

Clive and Patricia Morton have been sent by CMS to teach pastoral issues at a seminary in St Petersburg. They are working hard to learn Russian, and are learning how to engage with the different approaches to pastoral issues in a very different society. Clive will be lecturing on pastoral work and culture, and pastoral visiting, while Patricia will teach on AIDS and pastoral work.

These examples of working with the Orthodox Church remind us of the challenge of co-operating with other parts of the Christian Church. In many countries, the Church faces far bigger issues than differences of theological emphasis or church practice, and Christians have taken seriously Jesus' prayer in John 17:11 that his followers should be one. Within the Indian subcontinent, many of the Protestant denominations have combined to create United Churches. In China, what is known as a post-denominational Church has been established. These new churches challenge the Western mission agencies, with their denominational differences. Finding the right balance of ecumenical co-operation provides another tension within the task. Since 1986, there has been an ecumenical sending of English teachers to China, with CMS working with USPG (the United Society for the Propagation of the Gospel, another Anglican mission agency), the Methodist Church, the United Reformed Church, the Baptist Church, the Church of Scotland, and the Presbyterian Church of Ireland. A similar pattern of sending has evolved among some of these same churches, or agencies, in sending personnel to Bangladesh.

Faith and society

Given that evangelism and service are connected, many people find that it is still a big jump to accept that the gospel might challenge the structures of society. Acts 19:21–41 shows us that the two cannot be separated. In verse 21, we see that Paul thought his task in Ephesus was completed, and he was ready to move on to Jerusalem. The Holy Spirit had other plans for him: Paul had to learn the impact of his evangelism upon the local economy and society.

One of the local industries in Ephesus was the manufacture of silver shrines of Artemis (called Diana in some Bible translations), the local goddess. As more and more people moved from the worship of Artemis to Christianity, the silver shrine market collapsed and the silversmiths found their profits shrinking. One of the silversmiths, Demetrius, gathered all the others together to address the issue. His complaint was threefold. Firstly, their trade and therefore their pockets were being hit. Secondly, the reputation of the local temple was being diminished. This in turn would damage civic pride. Lastly, the goddess Artemis herself would lose her divine majesty. I find Demetrius refreshingly honest in the order in which he lists his complaints. Often people will talk first of the insult to their god, and then the insult to their nation, when what they are really concerned about is their income.

Authentic Christianity should always challenge the economy, culture, national identity and local gods of a community. Recent events in America, in which children have shot dead a number of their fellow pupils, have shown the strength of the gun lobby there. In Britain, the foxhunting lobby is powerful, and the tobacco industry and arms trades seem untouchable all over the world. Far be it from me to suggest which trades are not Christian—I am simply giving examples of powerful lobbies! But some exploitative industries, such as pornography and gambling, would vanish overnight if the whole population of a country embraced a Christian viewpoint.

On the other hand, Christianity should not seek to destroy a culture or try to replace it with the culture of another country. Christianity should bring the culture to true fulfilment. Jesus said, 'I have come that they may have life, and have it to the full' (John 10:10, NIV). The culture of the first Christians was clearly Jewish, but as Christianity engaged with the Greek-speaking world, the writers of the Epistles addressed and tried to fulfil the Greek culture rather than trying to impose a Jewish culture. Fulfilling a culture does still mean challenging some of its values and behaviour patterns, however, and as we do this we will encounter resistance, as there was in Ephesus when Paul was there.

Christianity was a threat to the false gods of Ephesus. We easily recognize the false gods within the culture of another faith, but we often ignore them or are blind to them within our own culture. Perhaps the Western 'false gods', including materialism, sexual freedom and jingoism, are not so different from those found in Ephesus.

Our first lesson from Acts 19 is that, if we are called into another society, we need to be aware of the ways in which Christianity might challenge that society's values. In order to do this, we need to understand how it challenges values within our own society. Otherwise, what hope do we have of understanding its effects in a new culture? As Christians we are called to be socially and politically aware. This means not only being interested in issues relating to personal ethics and morality, but trying to identify 'the principalities and the ruling forces' (Ephesians 6:12, NJB) that shape a society. We need to be aware of the root causes of poverty, unemployment, racism, divorce and the breakdown of the family both within our own society and elsewhere.

Different people will have different answers to these questions. I am not suggesting that there is only one Christian understanding of domestic and international issues, but being able to apply your faith to the issues within your own culture is a prerequisite for ministering within another culture.

There is also another lesson to learn: the appropriate response of ourselves as foreign visitors when Christianity does challenge the structures of the society in which we are called to serve. In Acts 19:30 we read that Paul wished to speak to the assembled crowd. Surely no one could be a better choice of spokesman than the foreign mission partner, articulate, with legal and religious training? But the local disciples do not allow Paul to speak upon this occasion. We are told (v. 33) that instead they pushed forward Alexander to speak, although the crowd (which by this time had become a mob) did not allow him a chance to speak. The implication is that Alexander was an Ephesian

Jew who had converted to Christianity. When the gospel started to challenge the structures of that society, leading to a riot, the local Christians decided that it was far more appropriate for a local believer to be in an upfront role than the foreign mission partner. This certainly backs up my own experience. I remember being on a visit to India and hearing about the work done by Christians addressing the plight of the exploited landless people in a particular village. The local Christians were not prepared to take me to that village, as it might have compromised their work, opening them to accusations that it was actually funded by foreigners who were challenging the structures of their society. If a foreign mission partner is politically active, the danger is that they will be perceived as an ambassador of their home country rather than an ambassador of Christ. An exception is where the challenge is to social structures imposed by white colonial nations. There was a very real role for foreign mission partners in challenging the apartheid regimes of southern Africa.

Another example of this kind of exceptional political involvement is the work of Marc Nikkel, an American Episcopal priest who served in Sudan for much of the 1980s and 1990s until his recent death after fighting cancer for two years. He had originally served in Sudan with the Episcopal Church of the United States of America (ECUSA). After going to live in Scotland for a few years, he felt led to return to Sudan and was sent jointly by CMS and his home diocese within ECUSA. Although his work was originally in theological education, his journeys into the devastation of the war-torn south of Sudan led the outside world to begin to take notice of what was going on there and even for some diplomatic pressure to be applied to the northern-based Sudanese government. Marc Nikkel's long-term involvement in Sudan meant that he was taken seriously by the different factions in the south, while maintaining independent status which enabled him to help negotiate peace talks between some of the groups involved.

NOTES
1   SCM Press, 1982
2   Regal Books Division, G/L Publications, 1973
3   The Koran, Surah V 110

CHAPTER 7

Called within a changing world

We live within a rapidly changing world. It has been said that the only thing that is now constant is change itself. Probably, not even this is true, as the rate of change itself appears to be increasing. In a world of rapid change, many are attracted to the security of Jesus Christ, who is described in Hebrews 13:8 as 'the same yesterday and today and for ever'. Although God himself and his love for his creation do not change, the ways in which God acts within his world might change, as might the way in which he asks his church to minister for him.

In the first chapter of this book we learned how God chose different representatives at different times in history to be the means of bringing his blessing to the nations. We saw, too, that those representatives had to re-evaluate their roles as the world around them changed and as their own understanding changed. Over the centuries, Christians have observed the world, looked afresh at their Bibles and gained new insights that have, from time to time, challenged traditional understanding. I present this chapter now, aware that because we all see the world in different ways some will disagree with my conclusions. And because of the speed of change, some of the views expressed here may well soon be out of date themselves!

The Great Commission

Despite such rapid change, many of those considering cross-cultural mission find their motivation in the same passage of scripture as their predecessors two hundred years ago. This starting point of Matthew 28:16–20, known as the Great Commission (or occasionally the alternative versions of the same events found in Acts 1:7–8 or Mark

16:15–20) may not change, but I suggest that our interpretation needs re-examining with time.

Let us look first at the most popular account, the one found in Matthew 28:16–20.

Now the eleven disciples went to Galilee, to the mountain to which Jesus had directed them. When they saw him, they worshipped him; but some doubted. And Jesus came and said to them, 'All authority in heaven and on earth has been given to me. Go therefore and make disciples of all nations, baptizing them in the name of the Father and of the Son and of the Holy Spirit, and teaching them to obey everything that I have commanded you. And remember, I am with you always, to the end of the age.'

Here Jesus commissions his remaining eleven followers to go and make disciples of all nations. We need to ask ourselves about the relevance of that Commission to us today. Who is Jesus really commissioning? Is it just those eleven men, or are you and I included, nearly two thousand years later—commissioned to take and preach the gospel throughout the world?

Before offering my answer, let us look at how the Great Commission has been interpreted by first considering Luke's account in Acts 1:6–8.

So when they had come together, they asked him, 'Lord, is this the time when you will restore the kingdom to Israel?' He replied, 'It is not for you to know the times or periods that the Father has set by his own authority. But you will receive power when the Holy Spirit has come upon you; and you will be my witnesses in Jerusalem, in all Judea and Samaria, and to the ends of the earth.'

Here the eleven disciples were instructed to wait until after the Holy Spirit came upon them. The events of Pentecost, described in Acts 2, brought about a great sharing of the gospel around Jerusalem. We have seen in the story of Philip that the Holy Spirit needed to disperse the early Christians in order to get the gospel out of Jerusalem, and a lot of work was needed to convince those early Jewish believers that the gospel was for the Gentiles as well as the Jews. Eventually the message was taken into the wider world. It certainly sounds as if the first disciples did not think that the Great Commission was aimed at them!

It is interesting to note the attitude of the early Protestants towards the Great Commission. This is summed up in the words of Johann Gerard, who died in 1637. He very clearly thought that 'the command of Christ to preach the Gospel to all the world ceased with the apostles; in their day the offer of salvation had been made to all the nations; there was no need for the offer to be made a second time to those who had already refused it.'

Robert Bellarmine, a noted Roman Catholic scholar writing in the late 17th century about the eighteen marks of the true Church, stated:

Heretics are never said to have converted either pagans or Jews to the faith, but only to have perverted Christians. But in this one century the Catholics have converted many thousands of heathens in the new world. Every year a certain number of Jews are converted and baptized at Rome by Catholics who adhere in loyalty to the Bishop of Rome; and there are also some Turks who are converted by Catholics both at Rome and elsewhere. The Lutherans compare themselves to the apostles and the evangelists; yet though they have amongst them a very large number of Jews; and in Poland and Hungary have the Turks as their near neighbours, they have hardly converted so much as a handful. [1]

The early Protestants, like the early Church at the time of the first disciples, had other issues to worry about. Until 1648 they were literally fighting for their lives, so they interpreted the Great Commission in a limited way. As we shall see later, it was only when the Western colonial expansion began in the 18th century that the Protestants rediscovered the Great Commission. Meanwhile, there had been Roman Catholic missionary work related to the Spanish and Portuguese colonial endeavours including South America, India and China.

We know from the account in Acts that the Commission would not come into effect until the coming of the Holy Spirit. Jesus' words in Acts 1:8 are a promise rather than a command, a promise which would be fulfilled with the gift of the Holy Spirit. And the Acts account tells how one further matter still needed to be sorted out after the Great Commission and before Pentecost. A twelfth apostle must be appointed to replace Judas. The fact that it is Matthias who is chosen, in verse 26, rather than Joseph called Barsabbas, seems immaterial. Neither of them are ever heard of again. What is important is that the apostles are twelve again, for within Hebrew tradition this is the number of completeness. There were twelve tribes of Israel, and Jesus deliberately chose twelve disciples to show that he represented the fulfilment of Israel. The completion of Christ's mission is symbolized by the advent of the new Jerusalem, described in Revelation 21:12–14, complete with twelve gates, twelve walls and twelve angels.

The fact that the Spirit does not come until the disciples are twelve again indicates that it is the whole body of Christ, the Church, that is being commissioned and not just a group of individuals. Israel had passed the missionary task of being a blessing to the nations to Jesus, who now passes the task to his Church.

There is a danger that we, with our individualistic Western culture, will interpret the passage to suit our circumstances, and assume that it is addressed to each of us personally, and not to the Church as a whole. Yes, of course the Commission is for us too, but we are commissioned as part of the Church made up of all Christians. All of us—not just those who feel that they have a special calling—are part of that commissioning. The responsibility for mission belongs not to individuals, but to the whole Church.

When we go abroad to share in another country's work of mission, if there is a church there the initiative and the invitation should come from the church of the receiving country. If there is no such invitation, there will have to be very good reasons for going there uninvited. And if we think that the church in another part of the world can gain from our contribution, can we also look at how we might benefit from their contribution to mission in our locality? Often, those who return from being involved in mission overseas are aware of how much their own culture could gain from the different Christian insights that they have heard elsewhere. Through the invitation of one church and the mission programme of another church, God still calls individuals to go and be involved in the work of the receiving church. What is important is that they see their role as being within the context of the whole body of Christ.

I have already mentioned that the early Protestant Church ignored the Great Commission until the late 18th century and the beginning of the great colonial expansion. Just as the early Church sent people to share the gospel with the Jews scattered through the Roman Empire, so did the churches of the Western colonial powers send clergy to minister to their own people in the colonies. Just as the Holy Spirit used the early Christians to reach the Gentiles, so the same Spirit used these clergy to reach the colonies. But by the end of the 18th century, God's initiative had become a human initiative. For better or for worse, the Great Commission was linked with the colonial expansion.

It was a time when Britain decided, 'All authority on earth has been given to me. Go therefore and make subjects of all nations; immersing them in the ways of the British, and teaching them to observe all the British laws. And know that the Empire will be with you always: yes, to the end of time.'

The British administrator overseas was told, 'You will receive power from the British navy, army and economy, and then you will be witnesses to what Britain stands for throughout Africa and Asia, and indeed to the ends of the earth.'

In Matthew's account of the Great Commission, the missionary is sent out with 'all authority in heaven and earth'—the authority of the Father. In Acts, it is with 'power when the Holy Spirit comes upon you'—the power of the Holy Spirit. The missionaries of the colonial era went out with this same authority and power. But to what extent did those to whom they went see that the authority and power were of God the Father and the Holy Spirit rather than of the colonial rule?

Christianity is now a world religion and the centre of Christendom has shifted away from Europe. There are now many Christians in the 'north' (the industrialized, wealthier countries from both hemispheres) and in the 'south' (the poorer, less developed countries). Although the colonial era has passed, we still have what is known as 'neo-colonialism', the economic and political dominance by the Western countries that impacts the governments of many developing countries. The colonial mentality can still be very much present among those who are themselves critical of it. It is easy to look critically at some of the legacies of Christian mission, such as church structures, centralized theological education and hospital-based medical work. It is easy for the Westerner to say, 'Although this is the model that we have in the West, it is an inappropriate one for your country and is purely a legacy of the colonial heritage. It needs modifying.' At one level this is a criticism of the colonial past; at another level it is an echo of it. Basically what is being said is, 'I, with my Western knowledge and background, know better than you what is best for you.'

Because the Great Commission has become so caught up with the secular authority and power of colonialism and neo-colonialism, should we then reject the Great Commission as no longer relevant? Many people do, and I have often heard, in Christian circles, mission being described as 'spiritual imperialism'. While this is a criticism that should be taken seriously, I feel that the answer lies in looking again at our Bibles. The version of the Great Commission found at the end of the Gospel of Mark is very similar to the versions that we have already been looking at, but John's version, found in John 20:20–23, has largely been ignored.

After he said this, he showed them his hands and his side. Then the disciples rejoiced when they saw the Lord. Jesus said to them again, 'Peace be with you. As the Father has sent me, so I send you.' When he had said this, he breathed on them and said to them, 'Receive the Holy Spirit. If you forgive the sins of any, they are forgiven them; if you retain the sins of any, they are retained.'

The disciples were sent out as the Father had sent Jesus. But how did the Father send Jesus? Jesus showing the disciples his hands and side—the marks of the nails in his hands and the wound of the sword in his side—sums up the nature of his sending. The Son was sent by way of incarnation to crucifixion. He was sent the way of the cross, the way of total vulnerability. Jesus sends his disciples, his Church, and us as part of that Church, in the same way.

- In Matthew the disciples are sent out with authority—the authority of the Father.
- In Acts they are sent out with power—the power of the Holy Spirit.
- In John they are sent out with vulnerability—the vulnerability of the Son.

We need to hold these three aspects of the Great Commission together in the same balance as they have within the Trinity. The Church is commissioned to go out with the authority of the Father, the power of the Holy Spirit and the vulnerability of the Son. If we emphasize one or two of these elements at the expense of the others, we can easily distort the good news that we have to share, and we are not being true to our understanding of a Trinitarian God.

If we emphasize power and authority at the expense of vulnerability, we can, as has already been shown, get confused with the power and authority of our nation, education or background. If we emphasize the vulnerability and forget about the authority, we can easily end up with a crisis of confidence in the whole concept of mission. We can over-emphasize the power of the Holy Spirit at the expense of the other elements, or we can get so caught up in the vulnerability and the authority that we forget that God does give us the very real power of the Holy Spirit.

The right balance among the three elements might depend upon our particular circumstances and also be shaped by what has gone before. Generally it is far easier for a Briton to speak as an equal with local Christians in a Francophone country where Belgium or France, rather than Britain, has been the colonial power. Prayerfully we can try to discern the Holy Spirit's leading in a particular situation. If in doubt, my advice is to remember the conclusion that Jesus reached in the wilderness, and opt towards vulnerability. Not only is it the example that Jesus gave us, but it allows the Spirit to take the initiative and show his power through our vulnerability.

Partnership

In our consideration of the Great Commission, we have looked at how God might call Christians from the Church in one place to go and share in the mission of the Church in another place. In the latter part of the 20th century, the word 'partnership' was increasingly used to describe such co-operation. We often act as if it was a 20th-century concept rather than a biblical one. Using different translations of the Bible, we find within the epistles Paul, Barnabas, James, Peter, John, Titus, Philemon, the readers of the letter to the Hebrews and Christ himself referred to as 'partners'. But it is Luke who first introduces us to the concept of partners, in his story of the calling of Simon (later Peter) and some of the other disciples in Luke 5:1–11.

As someone who is involved in testing calling, I am always interested in the processes used by others. What methodology will they use? In-depth interviews, references, written material, an affirmation of a particular statement of faith, psychiatric and medical assessment, personality tests or an assessment made from a role-play? Most organizations involved in testing vocation will use some combination of these methods. Jesus, when exploring the calling of his potential disciples, relied mainly upon the use of role-play. He set up a little exercise—a 'partnership test'—and ascertained how they responded to it.

In Luke 5:1–11, we see that first there is a brief test of the fishermen's response to authority. Despite their being tired and disillusioned about the prospect of further fishing (v. 4), they are asked to cast their nets again. They recognize the authority of Jesus and respond out of obedience (v. 5). So far, so good. Then, following Jesus' instructions, Simon and his companion find the fish and realize that they cannot land them all using their own strength (v. 6). The first stage of the partnership test is how they will respond to this need for extra help. They are aware of others who can help them, so they call out to these people to assist them with the task. Luke describes those to whom they appeal as their 'partners' (v. 7).

As we get to the end of verse 7, we begin to get into deep water—at least, the two sets of partners do. As they begin to work together, they all experience that sinking feeling—both those who called for help, and those who gave the help! Many who have worked in partnership in the tasks of mission will be familiar with that sinking feeling. The temptation is twofold. We can either conclude that partnership is too risky and that we should act on our own instead, or we can pretend that the risks are not there. If we take the first course of action, we are not following the biblical model and are unlikely to be successful in the task. We will also lose the opportunities to learn and grow as Christians that partnership offers us. If we glibly pretend that the risks are not there, then those who are experiencing and acknowledging the sinking feeling will feel that it is all their own fault. Who knows what damage this might cause them as individuals? We need to acknowledge that partnership can be difficult. And if we are forewarned, we can avoid some of the pitfalls or, at least, creatively work and grow through them.

What causes the sinking feeling? Let's imagine those two fishing boats working together, trying to land the one net. We know that the men had worked all night and were tired to begin with. We also know that the task was not an easy one—the catch was of an astonishing size. Both the size of the task and our human frailty can contribute towards that sinking feeling. I imagine that communication was also a factor. Did they have to establish who was telling whom what to do? Who had the authority to make the decisions at any point in the process? Communicating from one boat to another can provide opportunities for misunderstanding and, apart from any language difficulties, communicating from one culture to another can also cause misunderstanding.

Using this passage of scripture with our CMS mission partners-in-training, I have often posed the question, 'Why did the boats begin to sink?' In answer, I've heard the suggestion that the balance had changed. As one boat moved, the force of the heavy net upon each boat changed and the boats would have rocked. This is a very helpful insight into why those serving with another church might experience that sinking feeling. Partnership is not a static affair. It is a dynamic process and responsibilities will change at different times. It is often when a shift has taken place in the balance between the two partners that the sense of sinking is at its greatest.

Fishermen working together is one model of partnership but another useful one is marriage. Any marriage will go through a honeymoon period, when the partnership seems wonderful. This is followed by a time of getting used to each other, coming to terms with the fact that people see and express things in different ways and that this can cause misunderstanding. There is the realization that each partner has different strengths and weaknesses and habits that can annoy the other. The partnership survives and works as each partner learns not only about each other but also about themselves. This leads to growth, both in the two individuals and in the partnership itself.

To return to our Bible passage, the second part of the partnership test for the fishermen in the boats is how to respond to that sinking feeling. Simon is never one to bottle up his feelings. Will he blame his partners or will he blame Jesus? In fact, he blames himself. Simon falls at Jesus' knees (v. 8) and confesses his own sinfulness. His response to this part of the test is twofold: he worships Jesus and he admits his failings. It is when Simon has done this that Jesus, by saying, 'Do not be afraid; from now on you will be catching people' (v. 10), indicates that Simon has passed the partnership test and is right for the task of mission. Jesus is looking for those who, when they face that sinking feeling, can admit their weaknesses and confess their failings to Jesus. We also notice that this confession takes place in the presence of the other partners. It is no good admitting our failures to Jesus if we do not also tell the others who have been affected by those failures.

Obviously partnership is good for the soul but, we must ask ourselves, is it good for mission? In Luke 5:9 we are told that the partners were astonished at how many fish they had taken. Many fishermen are astonished at the size of the 'one that got away', but

Simon and his friends did manage to land the catch. We also know that it was a catch far bigger than any of them could have coped with alone. Partnership can work, but only if we work through that sinking stage. Jesus teaches us that as well as the other resources that he provides, he also offers us human partners. We will not always have the strength, insights or resources for the tasks of mission ourselves, and that is when we need to call others to help us.

Being a partner does not mean sailing into someone else's patch of water and taking over the fishing. It means responding to the call to go and help when your gifts are needed and requested. Partnership should also be mutual. We can assume from the story in Luke that the two boats were used to helping each other, and that sometimes it would be James and John who called to Simon to go and help them, reversing the initiative within the partnership. The success of a partnership lies with each partner recognizing their own strengths and weakness and the strength and weakness of their collaborators, so that they can mutually support one another. And the success of partnership also depends upon the relationship's being strong enough for each partner to be able to challenge the other.

When help is only ever requested by one partner, feeling that they have nothing to offer in return, then they are helpers rather than partners. In cross-cultural mission, each partner will have different insights and abilities. When we respond to Jesus' call to mission, we must bring together these insights and abilities in order to be effective in his task. It will not all be plain sailing but if we persevere, and work through the difficulties, God can achieve so much more than if we acted alone.

Multi-directional movements

When I first started work with CMS in 1980, I was told about 'Partners in Mission' consultations. The different Provinces of the Anglican Communion were encouraged to hold consultations on their mission and to invite some of their partners along, so that they could share their insights and possibly some help. By 1980 there were only two Provinces that had not yet had such consultations. One was Myanmar (formerly Burma), which was, and still is, a country quite closed to access and input from other countries. I was asked to guess which the other Province was. What other country was as closed to the outside world as Burma? Or if not actually closed, what other country was marked by extreme insularity in its views? I did not guess the right answer. Did you? It was the Church of England!

Sadly, because of the economic dominance of the West (or the North) in recent centuries, it is very easy for us to think of some nations as those that 'do' mission and others as those that 'receive' mission. This picture can be reinforced by the imagery of Matthew's account of the Great Commission. Jerusalem is the centre, sending out mission to Judea, Samaria and the ends of the earth. The West or North replaces Jerusalem in our picture, like the hub of a wheel with mission flowing out from the centre. But is this a true interpretation of the biblical model? Let us look at what happens in the Acts of the Apostles.

The first movement of Christians to other places was from Jerusalem, caused by scattering through Judea and Samaria (Acts 8:1) to escape persecution after the stoning of Stephen (Acts 7:55–60). Antioch then became the centre of missionary activity (Acts 11:19). The first deliberate sending of a Christian from one church to another was the initiative of the Jerusalem church, when it sent Barnabas to Antioch to encourage the Christians there (Acts 11:22). While the sending of the first person was from Jerusalem to Antioch, the first sending of financial resources was in the opposite direction. In response to a prophecy (Acts 11:27–30), the church in Antioch raised money and sent it to help the church in Jerusalem and Judea to cope with the coming famine.

Antioch became the church that sent, although it was a new church with a small leadership, and still had its own teaching task to complete. Nevertheless, the Holy Spirit indicated that Antioch should set aside Barnabas and Saul to be sent as missionaries (Acts 13:1–3). In any human strategy of mission, it would probably have been decided that Antioch was still a receiving church, in need of building up its own understanding of the gospel and developing a stronger leadership. Fortunately the strategy was in the hands of the Holy Spirit, and he was able to recognize and use the missionary zeal of the church in Antioch, which was prayerfully waiting for God's leading. The New Testament model is for each church to be both a sender and a receiver. At any point in time, each church will be blessed with certain people, gifts or insights which will need to be shared with other churches within the Christian body, as part of the task of mission. If a church is not aware of its need to learn and receive, it probably has very little to offer to other churches.

Paul develops this theme in Romans 12:4–8, with the imagery of different Christians with different gifts being part of the same 'body', all being dependent upon each other. His imagery applies equally to different churches in different parts of the world. Each has its own spiritual gifts and each can share with and learn from one another. In the last twenty years, CMS has begun to bring mission partners from churches overseas to serve in Britain and share their insights with the church here. Although we do still send far more mission partners than we receive, CMS now has more mission partners serving in England than in any other country!

In May 1997, the Church of Nigeria formed its own missionary society, CNMS (the Church of Nigeria Missionary Society). I was privileged to be invited to Nigeria that November to lead a workshop on selection and interviewing. It was exciting to catch some of their enthusiastic vision and their combination of prayerful hope and realism. Currently they are only sending people out within Nigeria, but they mean to extend their work soon to other parts of West Africa. They believe that all their mission partners should serve their first tour of service within Nigeria before being considered for service further afield. CMS is currently in conversations with CNMS to see if they could send a suitable mission partner to fill an opening in Asia that we have been unable to fill.

While I was in Nigeria, some colleagues of mine were at a consultation in Hong Kong which involved all of CMS's partners in South and East Asia. These were churches that had links to CMS but little or no contact with each other. The consultation helped to build an understanding not only of what mission might mean within another context, but also what resources they might have to share with each other. One practical response that has so far emerged is a joint initiative to address the needs of Filipino migrant workers in Hong Kong.

Shortly before this, CMS had been asked by the church of the Province of South Africa to send a mission partner with expertise on other faiths to be based in a parish with an Asian congregation. CMS could think of no obvious person to send and thought that it would make more sense if the person sent was Asian. In discussions with the Church of North India, a couple was identified and subsequently sent for the job. Both CMS and USPG were involved in this sending and receiving.

Since then, CMS has been involved in helping to facilitate other such people movements from one partner church to another. Currently the Episcopal Church in Egypt is asking CMS to send medical workers to the hospital that they run. This is so that they can send some of their workers to be involved in mission in other Arabic-speaking countries, where their detailed knowledge of language and culture could be crucial.

CMS is keenly aware of a bubbling up of the Holy Spirit, which is bringing more of these people movements into being. We are still seeking to establish what is the appropriate role for us to play in this exciting development. It is essential that anyone sensing a calling from a developed country to a developing country can see the bigger picture. Our Church is made up of interdependent parts, and the biblical pattern is that of multi-directional sending and receiving.

Enabling others

Missionary biographies make popular reading. It is possible from our Bibles to piece together potted biographies of some of the early missionaries. One of my favourites, who I feel is a real role model for our era but who often seems neglected, is Barnabas. His calling to mission is found in Acts 13, but we are first introduced to him in Acts 4:36 where his apparently generous act in selling a field and giving the money to the apostles seems to be taken for granted as expected of any believer. What is significant is his name. Barnabas is really named Joseph, a Levite from Cyprus, but he is known as Barnabas as this means 'son of encouragement'. What a lovely quality for others to see in him! If people gave you a name to reflect your qualities, what name would they give you? Can you think of a better name than to be called an encourager?

We next meet Barnabas in Acts 9:26–30, after Saul's conversion. Saul has had to flee for his life from Damascus and comes to Jerusalem to join the disciples. The disciples know of Saul from his pre-conversion days and do not trust him. They fear a trap. Could God really have converted such a man? For a moment, it appears that God's whole plan to work through Saul is about to be frustrated because of the disciples' lack of faith in God's power to convert. It is Barnabas, the encourager, who takes the risk and trusts Saul.

In trusting Saul, Barnabas is taking a step of faith and trusting God. God is able to see Saul not as he was, but as he might be under the influence of Christ's redeeming power. Barnabas believes the good that he has heard rather than the bad, and because of his trust the disciples accept Saul, enabling him to reach his full potential. Barnabas put himself out on a limb and took a big risk, personally. If he had not been prepared to do this, and if Saul had not been accepted and trusted, the whole early history of the Church could have been totally different.

In Acts 11:22–30, Barnabas is sent by the church in Jerusalem to the new and growing church in Antioch. Again his role is as an encourager. We are told in verse 23 how he encouraged them verbally. Barnabas also knew that the way to encourage a growing church was through teaching, and the best person to do the teaching would be Saul, so he fetched Saul to help with the task.

We read in Acts 12:25—13:3 that Barnabas and Saul are called by the Holy Spirit to service elsewhere. They leave behind a growing church with quite a small leadership, only five including Barnabas and

Saul. Often, leaders lack faith in those whom they lead and do not trust them to manage themselves. Barnabas' willingness to move on showed a confidence in those who were left behind which, in itself, would have been a further encouragement to them.

There is a subtle change in the ordering of the names from Acts 13:4 onwards. Until this point the reference has always been to Barnabas and Saul. In verse 4 it is to 'the two of them' (NIV). Later (v. 9) we are told that Saul is also known as Paul and by verse 13 the reference is to 'Paul and his companions'. Until this point, Barnabas has been the main character and Saul or Paul has been his companion; from here onwards, Barnabas takes a secondary role to enable Paul to develop his role. Anyone who encourages others will know that the encouragement of another person can easily have an impact upon one's own role. If we feel that we are the most important or that ours is the right way to do things, we will be setting up barriers that will stop us from truly encouraging others.

If this is true in our own culture, it can be even more the case within another culture. Often the role of the modern-day mission partner is to be a Barnabas—to be the encourager who enables the other to fulfil their potential while the mission partner moves out of the limelight. This becomes even more difficult if the sending church cannot understand and sympathize with such a role, and expects to hear stories of what the mission partner has done for the overseas church rather than what the overseas church is doing on its own account.

In Acts 15:36–41, Paul and Barnabas decide to revisit the churches that they have established. Barnabas wants to take Mark with them but Paul disagrees because Mark had deserted them at Pamphylia on the previous tour. This leads to a sharp disagreement and the parting of the ways for Paul and Barnabas. Once again it is Barnabas who puts his faith in someone that another will not trust. Barnabas looks for the potential that Mark might have, rather than judging him on his past experience.

This part of the story ends with Barnabas and Mark sailing off to Cyprus. Mark, whom Barnabas is prepared to trust, goes on to become a close companion of Peter in Rome, and the author of the earliest Gospel. Once again it looks as if Barnabas' judgment was correct, and we are left to speculate what might or might not have happened if Mark had been left behind by Barnabas, feeling useless and untrusted. Mark had made his mistake when he left them in Pamphylia. Perhaps Barnabas realized that people can learn and grow from their mistakes.

Many missionary biographies leave us impressed by the achievements of 'the Christian heroes of the past'. This is because our culture tends to judge people upon their achievements rather than their abilities to trust, relate, encourage and enable. The biography of a Barnabas may not make such exciting reading, but enabling and encouraging both Paul and Mark to move on and reach their full potential must have done more for the Kingdom than most people are able to achieve.

As Christianity has spread over the centuries to new countries and people-groups, those who have taken the gospel message have had to wrestle with the question of when and how to delegate responsibilities and when to let go. This issue of delegation has already been considered in Chapter 2, with the choosing of the first deacons in Acts 7. It provides an interesting insight not only into the outworking of delegation by the apostles, but also into how the Greek-speaking Christian community was involved in the processes at an early stage in the Church's growth. Henry Venn, General Secretary of CMS in the middle of the 19th century, concluded that every church should aim to be self-governing, self-financing and self-propagating. Such a model does not negate the interdependence of different parts of the Church or argue against partnership, but it does mean that the church in a particular place is responsible for its own mission and outworking of church life. The reality is that the dynamics of colonial domination, followed by the post-independence neo-colonial economic domination, means that this ideal is taking a long time to be achieved.

These days, anybody going to serve with a church in another country may find that church at any stage between a deep dependency upon the West and full independence. Whatever the stage of growth, it is important that the modern-day mission partner does not operate in a way that encourages dependence.

Foot-washing

There is a final issue related to ministry in a changing world that I would like to explore, which is demonstrated in the story of Jesus washing the disciples' feet (John 13).

Anyone who has served in an Islamic country or had much contact with Muslims will know not to put their Bible upon the floor, or let it make contact with feet. This attitude comes from an assumption that the Bible, as a holy book, should be treated with the same respect as the Koran. To the Muslim, the Koran is God's revelation and as such must be kept away from the dirtiness of feet, either through direct contact or indirectly through the floor or ground that has been subjected to the dirt of feet. To the Christian, of course, 'the Word became flesh and lived among us' (John 1:14): our primary revelation from God is not the Bible but Jesus himself.

That same Jesus is seen not avoiding the dirt of feet but actively seeking them out in order to cleanse them. I feel that this story of foot-washing holds together the heart of the gospel message. In the discussion between Jesus and Peter (John 13:6–13) it becomes obvious that the foot-washing is a sacramental act, an outward sign of an inner grace. The removal of dirt from the feet is a sign of the disciples being cleansed in a spiritual sense. Washing another person's feet is not a popular task: it is a messy job, involving kneeling on the floor, touching dirt, being splashed by dirty water and getting dirty oneself. This is why Jesus stripped off for the task. In taking away the disciples' uncleanness, Jesus takes some of their dirt upon himself. Jesus explains to Peter that unless he has his feet washed by Jesus, he can play no part in Jesus' work. Having made the disciples clean, Jesus instructs them, in turn, to be foot-washers.

The story shows Jesus as the incarnate servant, pointing out our need for cleansing, then cleansing us and instructing us to join him in the role of servanthood and the work of cleansing. Both baptism and the atoning work upon the cross are symbolized by what happens. Our adoption as his heirs is there in our qualifying, through the cleansing, to be a part of him. The responsibility that we have to be servants, and to be part of the mission of cleansing a sinful world, is there within the instruction to wash the feet of others (John 13:13–14). This apparently simple story in fact embraces the whole essence of the Christian message of incarnation, baptism, atonement and the life within the Church.

What we so often forget is the fact that in the act of cleansing Jesus takes on some of our dirt. If we engage with the sin of the world, we too can expect to pick up some dirt. It is easy to point out dirt without coming into contact with it, but we cannot be involved in the task of cleansing without some risk that we will get dirty ourselves.

I remember a mission partner in India explaining in a letter that a Hindu lady had reprimanded him. He had attended a Hindu celebration and she had felt that his mission agency would be angry with him for doing so. He had wanted to try to understand more deeply what Hinduism was about and what it meant to a Hindu. To do so, he needed to experience that particular ceremony. Afterwards he was not so sure that it was such a good idea, but he felt that God honoured his motivation and if it was a sin, it would be forgiven.

A few years ago, I was shown around a fascinating community in Hong Kong. It was originally a Buddhist monastery that had converted, some decades previously, to Christianity. It is now used as a resource centre for exploring an engagement with other faiths. It is the type of place that would unsettle many Christians, as the Buddhist imagery is there within the chapel. The altar looks typically Buddhist in style and the baptismal font has the motif of the water-lily, a Buddhist symbol of purity, carved on it. None of the group that I was with reacted against the imagery or other aspects of this centre. The director who showed me around spoke honestly and openly about the tension involved in a serious engagement with other faiths and how, at times, they had probably got it wrong and gone too far.

I have read the testimony of a church leader who needed to guide his church through a time of severe persecution. If the church held totally true to all that it believed in, then it could either be so persecuted that it would cease to exist or be driven so deeply underground that it would no longer be noticed. If it was prepared to compromise upon certain issues, it could survive and publicly witness on the issues upon which it had not compromised. That church grew during that time because of the witness that it was able to make. The leader felt, in retrospect, that some of the decisions he had made might not have been the right ones. He had simply been seeking a way to witness effectively to the gospel, and there was an openness before God and the rest of the Christian community that some of the decisions might end up being the wrong ones.

In the same way, Christians of all generations have had to engage with the society to which they are trying to witness. They have needed to follow Jesus' example of incarnational living and to work hard to understand how others perceive issues. Within our ever-changing world, Christians will be called to more and more situations where, in order to have a chance of cleansing the dirt, we will risk getting mucky ourselves. The good news is that we can do so in the confidence that we are following the command of Jesus and that he is still there to cleanse us.

NOTE
1   Both quotes from 'A History of Christian Missions', Stephen Neill, *The Pelican History of the Church 6*, Pelican, 1964

CHAPTER 8

God, me, the Church and the world

We have considered a God who can be experienced within our deepest being, within our feelings, guiding our thought processes as we make sense of the world and of our experiences—a God with whom we need to wrestle, and who enables us to grow. We have looked, too, at a God who acts out there in the world; the God who loves us and the rest of his creation so much that he has taken the initiative to restore the relationship between himself and his creation and all of the nations; the God who sends others to restore the relationship with him and also to restore all those other broken relationships within his world. We have considered a God who might challenge us through the needs that we see within the world; a God who is Lord of all cultures and who might excite us by what we learn about him and ourselves when we enter different cultures; a God who sends his Holy Spirit to guide those who struggle with the tensions of the task; a God who sends the Holy Spirit to stimulate new responses in the task of mission and ministry in every age.

God in history

The big question is whether or not I can hold together the God I experience within myself with the God I experience out there in the world. Can I reconcile Jesus, as my personal saviour, with the cosmic Christ who is in control of history? If I believe that God knows me and cares for me and has plans for what I do with my life, can I believe that the same God is able to respond in the same way to the whole of his creation? If I believe in a God who does work within his whole creation, can I believe that he has the time and energy to take an intimate interest in little old me, and feel that he can use me in some way within his plans?

The answer to all of these questions must be yes, but it is beyond any human understanding to know how it could be done. We need the Holy Spirit to begin to bridge the gap from one way of understanding to another. Like Job, we can be so caught up in our own situation that we are blinded to the bigger picture. If you feel like that, then read those last five chapters of Job, where God puts Job's concerns into their true context within the bigger picture of his creation. Another passage that presents us with the big picture is Psalm 24. It is, of course, preceded by Psalm 23, with the assurance of God's love and concern for the individual. This in turn is preceded by Psalm 22, which captures the essence of the cross and bridges the gap from the wrestling of the individual to the wonders of God's plan for his whole creation.

God can bring good out of disaster in our own individual lives. Where can we find that same God at work in world history? My starting point is that I believe in Jesus as my personal Saviour; yet he also died and rose again to redeem the whole creation. I do not believe that God makes disasters happen, but I believe that God can bring good in the lives of individuals out of disasters and misfortunes. I also believe that, ultimately, God is in control of history and to believe this we have to have a long-term view of events. A helpful passage to consider in this context is Acts 16:6–10, when Paul is forbidden from taking the gospel to Asia, but instead has a vision to go to Macedonia. If God wanted Paul to share the gospel in Macedonia rather than Asia, we should ponder what the long-term consequences of this guidance have been.

As a European, I am biased. Paul saw his calling as sharing the gospel in Asia and not in Europe. Personally I am very pleased that God made Paul bring the gospel into Europe. The fact that I, a European, am a Christian today might be a result of Paul's being turned away from Asia. The place where Paul wanted to preach the gospel is now within an area that is solidly Islamic. The majority of Christians now in Macedonia will be Orthodox Christians. The missionary movement of the Orthodox Church was in a northerly direction through the Balkans, with the Church finally being established in Russia over a thousand years ago. By the time that Greece and the Balkans lost their Christian influence to the power of the Islamic Ottoman Empire, the Orthodox Church was firmly established in Russia. Russia, in turn, was to lose the authority of the Orthodox Church for over 70 years after the Communist revolution in 1917. But by 1918, the influence of the Ottoman Empire had ended in Greece and the Balkans and they were free to be Christian again. With the benefit of hindsight, we can see that God has been in control. The flame of Eastern Orthodoxy was not allowed to be extinguished.

Returning to Paul's story, we are aware that for much of the time that he might have been evangelizing new areas, he was in prison. How did Paul feel about this? How did he see God in what was going on in his life? While Paul was in prison, he wrote letters to many of the new churches that he had founded. Many of those churches have not survived, but have been swept away by the rise of Islam. What survived were some of those letters of Paul, and the influence that they have made upon Christian thinking and understanding. At the time of his death, Paul would have had no idea of what God would achieve in the long term through his work, but he knew that God was in control even though it did not appear obvious at the time.

For many years, it was nearly impossible for missionaries to go to serve in India. The Church in India was asking for them to come but the Indian government would not issue visas. The lack of Western missionaries made the Indian Church far more dependent upon its own resources and helped it to grow in confidence. It is now far more aware of what it has to offer to the churches of the West, and in its relationship with those churches we see equality rather than dependence.

In pre-Communist China there was a saying that 'one Christian more means one Chinese less'. Christianity was so tied up with out-side influences that converts were seen as losing their Chinese identity on becoming Christian. The foreign Christians all had to leave shortly after the Communist revolution, and the remaining Christians were often persecuted, particularly during the years of the Cultural Revolution. Their ability to cope with persecution was a witness that impressed many. As China has emerged from that period of repression, it is obvious that not only has the Church in China grown tremendously in numbers but also that without Western contact it has become authentically Chinese. Many of those who were expelled from China in the 1950s died before they could see the resurrected Church that had emerged in China. Others were fortunate enough to see confirmation that God was in control.

The late Bishop Lesslie Newbigin, one of the foremost missionary thinkers and writers of the last century, was often asked, while serving in India, if he was optimistic about mission. He replied that he knew that Jesus had been crucified and had risen again. Christ's victory has happened. It is not something that we have to be optimistic or pessimistic about. We may stop the clock of history on a particular event and only see crucifixion and death. If we allow the clock to run, then in God's good time we will see resurrection and new life. With certain events in history, the clock will stop on us and we will not, in this life, see resurrection. But if we have a proper understanding of the resurrection, we will know that God is in control, the battle has been won and that, ultimately, death is followed by resurrection and new life.

Being the Church

As individuals, we may gain new and exciting understandings of how God is working within his world. It is essential that these insights are integrated into the thinking of the Church. I return to the story of Peter and Cornelius to make the point. This time we look at what happened next—the continuation of the story within Acts 11:1–18.

I do not know what sort of system Peter had for distributing his prayer letters, but there must have been some effective means of communication, as everyone in Judea was aware of what he had been up to. When he returned to Jerusalem after his encounter with

Cornelius, he was soon in trouble. All the circumcised believers criticized him for mixing with the wrong type of people.

There were two separate but related issues at stake here. First, the social issue mentioned at the beginning of Acts 11: Peter had mixed with the 'wrong type' of people, with Gentiles, bringing them into the Church. The deeper issue was a theological one. Peter had discovered (Acts 10:34–35) that God's plans for mission and salvation were bigger than he had realized. The Church had not yet taken on that new understanding. These eighteen verses in Acts 11 make it sound as if the issue of who could and could not become Christians, and what was required of them, was sorted out very easily. A careful reading of Acts and some of the Epistles will show us that this issue took a while to be resolved. At the start of Acts 10 there is a very real danger that Christianity will remain just another Jewish sect, whereas by the start of Acts 11 the danger is that the Church will divide in two—a Jewish Church and a Gentile Church. The danger of such a split repeats itself during the first few decades of the early Church, and the pattern has continued through history.

There is a tension built into the very nature of the Church. If it never reaches out to different cultures, then it will never have to engage with different types of people. By its very nature, the Church should be a missionary Church, and its missionary task brings some Christians into contact with very diverse people-groups with their own cultures and philosophies. As the gospel is related to these people, and to their worldview, the Christian understanding of God's love and purposes within salvation grows. The larger Church, without the first-hand experience of seeing the Holy Spirit at work in the situation, may struggle to accept either the people-group or the new understanding of God. The temptation is always to split and form different Churches.

Although the Church comes close to splitting during the era of Acts and the Epistles, it is prevented from doing so by the Holy Spirit. In Acts 11 Peter tells his story, which we have already read twice before in Acts 10. In the space of a chapter and a half, we have this story three times. This does not indicate bad editing, but shows the importance of the story to the future life of the Church. What is lost to the modern reader is the significance of the six men who were with Peter (v. 12). In Egyptian and Roman law, a point would be proved beyond doubt if there were seven male witnesses. The Holy Spirit had provided Peter with just the right number of additional witnesses for the events to be accepted as fact.

If you are called to any ministry, and particularly cross-cultural mission, God may give you new insights. What is essential is that these are tested within the Church and also integrated into the Church. This might not happen immediately but you should keep working at it! If the new insights are of the Holy Spirit, the Holy Spirit will find ways of unifying those insights into the Church.

How does God move people?

We have looked at how people within the Bible have been called. We have looked at the type of tasks to which they have been called and at some of the issues that might need exploring as a result. For many people, the real question will be whether or not they are being called. How do we really know?

Imagine the scenario given below. There are three different countries—A, B and C. They might or might not be adjoining each other.

What are the different ways in which someone might move from country A to country B? I think that there are six reasonably distinct ways in which this might happen. Although the example is about moving from one country to another, I think that the conclusions are equally valid for a move to ministry within your own country:

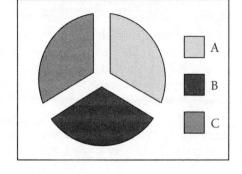

- To help: Someone in B asks someone in A to come and help them; or someone in C, aware of a need in B, suggests to someone in A that they go and help them.
- To learn: Someone in B asks someone in A to come and learn from them.
- Obedience: Someone, possibly God, tells someone from A to move to B.
- To represent: The people of A send one of their number as a representative to B.
- Profit: As part of their profession, someone from A visits or goes to work in B.
- Persecution: Either the people of C, or a subgroup of the people of A, terrorize some people from A so that they are forced to go and live in B; or else the people from B go and bring back as captives some people from A.

I want to look primarily at the first four of these, but the last two demand some consideration first.

Persecution

While the Bible, church history and biographies will mention the individuals who were called to cross cultural boundaries to do mission, the vast majority of missionary activity has probably been carried out by those who moved out of a sense of terror. It was the persecution following the martyrdom of Stephen that led to Christianity moving outside Jerusalem, and it was one of those dispersed communities, the church in Antioch, that was involved both in sharing their faith locally and with sending Barnabas and Saul.

I do not believe that God creates disasters so that people will become refugees, but I do believe that God has worked through such movements over the years, bringing good out of bad. One current example is the Karen refugees, a Christian minority from Burma now living in Thailand, and also the Sudanese refugees spread around a whole host of countries.

Profit

Another anonymous category of missionary is the trader, or anyone who moves from one country to another through their employment. Again God has often used such people, and continues to do so, as a means of sharing the gospel. (I am not including within this type of movement those known as 'tentmakers'. 'Tentmakers' are primarily those who have a sense of calling from God to another country, and use their trade as a means of supporting themselves.) I am thinking of those whose primary motivation is where they can best carry out their livelihood but who witness to their faith in the place where their livelihood takes them. CMS has a programme known as the Salt Fellowship, described in the Appendix on page 140, which is for those in just such positions.

Now let us look at the four remaining ways in which people are moved, and test them against some of the biblical stories that we have considered.

To help

We have considered some of those who were summoned to join in the task—the two disciples asking their partners to help them fish, Cornelius inviting Peter, and also Paul's vision of the Macedonian asking for help. As a Roman citizen, Paul had the right to cross many national boundaries. Thankfully, the era has passed when a British passport worked in the same way. If you are going to live in another country, you will not be allowed to work there unless someone, or some institution, has asked you. So, this call to move is in two parts: there must be some task that needs to be carried out *and* there must be an invitation for you to go and fulfil that task.

To learn

In our second example, someone asks you to come so that you can learn something from them. Peter came to a new and far deeper understanding of Christianity through the conversion of Cornelius, and Apollos had to learn all about the Holy Spirit from the local Christians in Ephesus. Jonah had to learn about compassion, and all of the characters that we have looked at have had to be open to growing as people and in their understanding of God. Hosea was a particularly good example of someone becoming better able to understand God through his own difficult experiences. Nowadays people might be stimulated to learn more about God by seeing him at work in a different culture or by exploring some of the tensions of the tasks of ministry and mission.

Obedience

Our third example concerns those who are told to move. Obedience to God's leading is a common theme that runs through the different stories that we have looked at. As we have seen, different people will hear God's voice in different ways. The important thing is the conviction that it is God that we are obeying. The biblical examples that we have considered have included some people in very difficult circumstances. That has not changed. If you are called to cross-cultural service today, you can expect to find yourself facing difficulties and uncertainties. Like Jeremiah, you might experience self-doubt. What keeps people going through such difficult times is the certainty that they are where God wants them to be. They have a certainty that they are being obedient.

To represent

In our fourth example, a person is sent as a representative of others. In studying the Great Commission, we have seen that the call is not to individuals but to the whole Church. In Acts 6, the seven deacons were delegated by the wider Church and given particular tasks. They were chosen as representatives and seemed to have very little say in the matter themselves. The same is true of Barnabas and Saul, chosen as representatives of the church in Antioch, after prayer and fasting. We can assume that prayer did not end with their selection! Anybody going into mission needs to be sure that there will be prayer support both through a congregation and the wider Church or mission agency.

Through our baptism we are all called to be involved in the ministry and mission of the Church. Not all of us need to move from one place to another to be part of that ministry. If God wants us to move to do a particular task in a particular place as part of his mission, there will be a sense of calling. While any of the four methods discussed above can be used to move someone from one place to another, I feel that all four are essential elements of a modern-day Christian calling.

The order in which I have expressed the methods of calling is random. For some people, it will start with the awareness of need and a response to that. For others, it will be the desire to learn and grow and to engage with new people, new cultures and new issues. Others will start with a sense that it is God's prompting, and an exploration of that prompting will lead to a certainty and to obedience. Still others will start with a sense of having been encouraged by their fellows and set aside by the wider body as representatives to carry out a particular task. Our personalities, our culture, our church backgrounds and understanding of Christian teaching might all influence how we function and how we perceive God communicating to us.

Exploring a calling is an invitation to wrestle with God. We may be hurt; we may, as with a dislocated hip, need to tackle the root of that hurt. Jacob was hurt by God and also blessed by God. Ultimately, if we feel called to explore how we can be a blessing to the nations, then, like Jacob, we will be blessed by God.

Appendix

CMS UK Personnel Programmes

CMS works in partnership with churches in Africa, Asia, Britain, Eastern Europe and the Middle East. To enable this, we have the following mission personnel programmes:

Mission partners: Mission partners are sent in response to specific requests by a partner church for people to bring certain professional skills as well as their commitment to mission. In order to engage with the language and culture, most openings require a minimum of four to six years' service but a few openings are possible with a two- or three-year commitment. Currently there are about 150 mission partners, and we have approximately 50 vacancies. The majority have gone out from Britain, but those serving in Britain have mainly been recruited from partner churches.

Make a Difference: Overseas placements are for those in the 21–30 age range and British placements are for the 18–30 age range. Placements are for those looking for a cross-cultural experience and a way of developing spiritually through contact with the Church overseas or in Britain. Placements last 6 to 18 months. A similar programme is being developed for those with professional experience, including the retired and early retired.

Encounter: This consists of groups of about ten people in the 18–30 age range going with two experienced leaders for three or four weeks to live alongside Christians in partner churches. It is an opportunity to share in their lifestyle, witness, worship, hopes and aspirations. Each year we send out four or five groups. Young people from partner churches come to Britain on *Encounter Britain*.

Praxis: This consists of groups of no more than ten people, aged over 25, led by an experienced leader together with a national chaplain, offering a time of spiritual refreshment and intellectual challenge as group members engage with the issues facing the local Christian community and reflect upon their experiences. Visits are for two or three weeks.

Salt Fellowship: This is for people who are working abroad in roles that, usually, they have found for themselves. These roles need to be in countries where CMS relates to the Church, and must also reflect the priorities of CMS. Participants are expected to relate closely and creatively to the churches where they are and to the Church in the UK. CMS offers advice, local contacts, prayer support and opportunities for preparation and reflection.

Bible college placements: We are able to arrange a limited number of three-month cross-cultural placements with partner churches, for those studying at Bible colleges.

Ministerial training electives: These are designed for those who have been accepted to train for the ministry. A placement of three months, experiencing the issues faced by the Church in another culture, can add a new dimension to future ministry.

Sabbaticals: These are opportunities for clergy to learn and gain from a stay of about three months with a partner church.

CMS covers the cost of preparation and group reflection for these mission programmes. Mission partners are supported on allowances. The other programmes are basically self-funding but advice can be given on fund-raising and some assistance can be provided for sabbaticals, ministerial training electives and the 6–18 month placements for those with professional skills.

CMS can consider those from outside Britain only if the initiative comes from their national church. The *Interchange*, *South to South*, *Everywhere2Everywhere* and *Scholarship* programmes provide opportunities for experience, service and study for those from partner churches.

Further information from Personnel Programmes Team, CMS, Partnership House, 157 Waterloo Rd, London SE1 8UU. Tel: 020 7928 8681; fax: 020 7401 3215. E-mail: programmes.manager@cms-uk.org; Website: www.cms-uk.org

Sister societies

CMS Ireland
Church of Ireland House
61–67 Donegall Street
Belfast
BT1 2HQ
Tel: 02890 324581
E-mail: cmsibelfast@ireland.anglican.org
Website: www.cmsireland.org

CMS Australia
93 Bathurst Street
Sydney
NSW 2000
Australia
Tel: 020 9284 6777
Fax: 02 9267 3626
E-mail: federal@cms.org.au
Website: www.cms.org.au

CMS USA
62 East Grand Avenue
New Haven
CT 06513
USA

New Zealand CMS
CMS House
167 Wairakei Road
Christchurch 8005
New Zealand
Tel: +64 3 351 6415
Fax +64 3 351 5987
E-mail: office@nzcms.org.nz
Website: www.nzcms.org.nz

Other Anglican mission agencies mentioned in this book

Crosslinks
251 Lewisham Way
London
SE4 1XF
Tel: 020 8691 6111
Fax: 020 8694 8023
E-mail: mission@crosslinks.org
Website: www.crosslinks.org

South American Mission Society (SAMS)
Personnel, Unit 11
Prospect Business Park
Langston Rd
Loughton
Essex
IG10 3TR
Tel/Fax: 020 8502 3504
E-mail: persec@samsgb.org
Website: www.samsgb.org

United Society for the Propagation of the Gospel (USPG)
Partnership House
157 Waterloo Rd
London
SE1 8XA
Tel: 020 7928 8681
Fax: 020 7928 2371
E-mail: enquiries@uspg.org.uk
Website: www.uspg.org.uk

Other UK mission agencies and churches mentioned in this book

Baptist Missionary Society (BMS)
PO Box 49
Baptist House
Didcot
Oxon
OX11 8XA
Tel: 01235 517700
Fax: 01235 517601
E-mail: kkavanagh@bms.org.uk
Website: www.bms.org.uk

Church of Scotland
World Mission
121 George Street
Edinburgh
EH2 4YN
Tel: 0131 225 5722
E-mail: world@cofscotland.org.uk
Website: www.churchofscotland.org.uk

Methodist Overseas
World Church Office
25 Marylebone Road
London
NW1 5JR
Tel: 020 7486 5502
Website: www.methodist.org.uk

United Reformed Church
International Relations
86 Tavistock Place
London
WC1H 9RT
Tel: 020 7916 8654
E-mail: international@urc.org.uk
Website: www.urc.org.uk

Useful contacts

There are plenty of other mission agencies not mentioned here. Both of the following produce publications listing the openings of, and useful information about, a number of different mission agencies. Both these agencies also offer a vocational interview service.

Christian Vocations
St James House
Trinity Road
Dudley
West Midlands
DY1 1JB
Tel: 01384 233511
E-mail: info@christianvocations.org
Website: www.christianvocations.org

Christians Abroad
Room 233
Bon Marché Centre
241–251 Ferndale Rd
London
SW9 8BJ
Tel: 020 7346 5957
E-mail: projects@cabroad.org.uk
Website: www.cabroad.org.uk

Vocational conferences

With an emphasis upon cross-cultural mission:

Fit for the Purpose: These are weekend events run by St John's Extension Studies based upon the workbook of the same name. They offer an opportunity to explore a wide range of Christian ministries. Details and workbooks from St John's Extension Studies, Bramcote, Nottingham NG9 3RL. Tel: 0115 925 1117; Fax: 0115 943 6438; Email: ext.studies@stjohns-nottm.ac.uk. St John's Extension Studies also produce two other workbooks that are recommended to those considering cross-cultural mission: *The World Christian* and *Entering Another's World*.

Partnership for World Mission will be able to provide information about any vocational events that the Anglican mission agencies are involved in. Information from PWM Office, Partnership House, 157 Waterloo Rd, London SE1 8XA.
Tel: 020 7803 3201; Email: sally.smith@c-of-e.org.uk

CMS are from time to time involved in running or taking part in vocational events. Details from Personnel Programmes Team, CMS, Partnership House, 157 Waterloo Rd, London SE1 8UU.
Tel: 020 2928 8681; E-mail: programmes.manager@cms-uk.org;
Website: www.cms-uk.org

Which Way? These day events are organized by Christian Vocations and explore subjects like guidance, gifting and opportunities. Details from Christian Vocations, St James House, Trinity Road, Dudley, West Midlands DY1 1JB.

Tel: 01384 233511; E-mail: info@christianvocations.org;

Website: www.christianvocations.org

With an emphasis upon Anglican ministries:

There are a number of such events. Up-to-date details can be obtained from The Ministry Division, Archbishops' Council, The Church of England, Church House, Great Smith Street, London SW1P 3NZ. Tel: 020 7898 1399; Website: www.cofe.anglican.org

Bible colleges

There are over forty of these in Britain. Workers currently either serving, or in contact with, CMS include people who have been to the following:

All Nations Christian College	London Bible College
Easneye	Green Lane
Ware	Northwood
Herts	Middlesex
SG12 8LX	HA6 2UW
Tel: 01920 461243	Tel: 01923 45 6000
Fax: 01920 462997	Fax: 01923 45 6001
E-mail: mailbox@allnations.ac.uk	E-mail: cms@londonbiblecollege.ac.uk
Website: www.allnations.ac.uk	Website: www.londonbiblecollege.ac.uk

Redcliffe College
Wotton House
Horton Road
Gloucester
GL1 3PT
Tel: 01452 308097
Fax: 01452 503949
E-mail: admin@Redcliffe.org
Website: www.Redcliffe.org

Further details about the full range of Bible colleges is available from Christian Vocations (details as above).